MODERN NINJA WARFARE

Ninja Tactics for the Modern Warrior

Antony Cummins

T0161030

TUTTLE Publishing

Tokyo │Rutland, Vermont│ Singapore

ABOUT TUTTLE
"Books to Span the East and West"

Our core mission at Tuttle Publishing is to create books which bring people together one page at a time. Tuttle was founded in 1832 in the small New England town of Rutland, Vermont (USA). Our fundamental values remain as strong today as they were then—to publish best-in-class books informing the English-speaking world about the countries and peoples of Asia. The world has become a smaller place today and Asia's economic, cultural and political influence has expanded, yet the need for meaningful dialogue and information about this diverse region has never been greater. Since 1948, Tuttle has been a leader in publishing books on the cultures, arts, cuisines, languages and literatures of Asia. Our authors and photographers have won numerous awards and Tuttle has published thousands of books on subjects ranging from martial arts to paper crafts. We welcome you to explore the wealth of information available on Asia at **www.tuttlepublishing.com**.

Published by Tuttle Publishing, an imprint of Periplus Editions (HK) Ltd.

www.tuttlepublishing.com

Copyright © 2019 Antony Cummins

Library of Congress Control Number: 2019938001

ISBN: 978-4-8053-1481-4

First edition
22 21 20 19   5 4 3 2 1   1905RR
Printed in China

TUTTLE PUBLISHING® is a registered trademark of Tuttle Publishing, a division of Periplus Editions (HK) Ltd.

Distributed by

North America, Latin America & Europe
Tuttle Publishing
364 Innovation Drive
North Clarendon, VT 05759-9436 U.S.A.
Tel: (802) 773-8930
Fax: (802) 773-6993
info@tuttlepublishing.com
www.tuttlepublishing.com

Japan
Tuttle Publishing
Yaekari Building, 3rd Floor 5-4-12 Osaki
Shinagawa-ku, Tokyo 141 0032
Tel: (81) 3 5437-0171
Fax: (81) 3 5437-0755
sales@tuttle.co.jp
www.tuttle.co.jp

Asia Pacific
Berkeley Books Pte. Ltd.
3 Kallang Sector #04-01, Singapore 349278
Tel: (65) 6741-2178
Fax: (65) 6741-2179
inquiries@periplus.com.sg
www.periplus.com

TABLE OF CONTENTS

SAFETY NOTE

The techniques in this book can cause severe bodily injury and even death. The ability to do bodily damage and to kill—and to train others in techniques that may do so—imposes grave responsibilities. The potentially lethal techniques in this book should never be used except for defensive purposes in the most extreme life-and-death situations. Knowledge of these techniques requires high levels of maturity and responsibility, and no one who lacks such maturity should be using this book at all.

The techniques in this book should be practiced only in consultation with a trained martial arts teacher who can provide advice about their safe and responsible use. The physical activities described in this book are strenuous and should not be attempted by anyone who is not in good physical health. The author and publisher disclaim responsibility for any harmful effects, on yourself or others, whether intended or unintended.

PREFACE

When my editor at Tuttle Publishing, Jon Steever, first approached me and asked if I would like to write a modern book on the shinobi, I was extremely hesitant. Often, such books move into fanciful directions, based on a very poor understanding of shinobi history. However, his letter contained the baited sentence "you are at the top of our list to write this book." I realized that if I said no, then another book of "super-ninja" caliber would be added to the already vast stack in existence. Therefore, with reluctance at the start, I buckled down and set to work on finding the heart of a comparison between the old and the new. It is with great pleasure that I now have to thank Jon because this book was a pleasure to research. Also it has become a volume that will allow both the shinobi and modern Special Forces community to come together and appreciate the depth of the expertise found in both camps.

I truly hope that after reading this book that your understanding of the shinobi and modern Special Forces will have been expanded and that you will have found a new respect for their shadowy world that lies beyond the public view, either in days gone by or in the most dangerous places upon the earth today. I would also request for the covert operations community to join in friendship and to help preserve Japanese culture by taking an active interest in the ancient and wise ways of the shinobi and that you will allow me to ask for your support in keeping both Japanese and shinobi culture alive.

Antony Cummins
2019

Never was espionage carried out in such perfection as it was in Japan.

—Lord Redesdale 19th century

Author's Note:
You Have Been Warned

*y*ou should be well aware of the dangers of both this book's contents as well as the many ways the ninja are misunderstood. Therefore the following text will help you to form the proper mindset before you delve deeper.

Do Not Try This at Home

This book contains extremely dangerous and violent content. The author and the publisher both insist that nothing from this publication be used in real life situations and should be considered to be an overview of covert operations both historical and contemporary. Any instructional statements such as "you should do this" is simply a stylistic approach with the understanding that it represents a hypothetical situation directed towards a ninja of old or a Special Forces member of today. Special Forces and paramilitary members today already have their skill-sets and much of the information in this book could be considered both illegal and immoral. Furthermore, we cannot turn back time. The ninja of old are long gone and their methods here are presented for the enjoyment of history lovers. It is with great seriousness that I say *"do not try this at home."*

An Overview of Historical Ninja Research

For those readers who are not familiar with my work, I am an English author based in Britain and (at times) Japan. I have dedicated my life to the accurate understanding of Japanese military culture, especially the ninja. I am the project leader of a small group that is dedicated to the production of English translations of real and historical ninja scrolls. Our aim is to provide correct information and historical accuracy based on original ninja manuscripts and primary documents. To date, as a team we have translated and published many ninja manuals and books on ninja skills—as full

translations, as historical investigation and as easily accessed illustrated guides to historical ninja. For more information on the books produced by the team (see page 181).

The author, Antony Cummins, in the Japanese National Archives with one of the original transcriptions of the famous ninja manual *Bansenshukai* (1676), which the team translated and published as *The Book of Ninja*.

Illustrations in This Book

The illustrations in this book provided by Jay Kane are only guidelines and are included for "flavor." Much of the tools, weapons and equipment are illustrated by using vector files and may not represent accurate technology or be historically accurate. Consider these images as guides to help bring illustrate each topic but should not be considered true to life.

Japanese Terms and Original Quotes

Japanese terms in this book have been reduced to a minimum and all macrons have been removed, therefore, Tōkyō becomes Tokyo. This has been done for all terms. Japanese names have been given as family first and given name second.

This book gives quotes from original samurai and ninja scrolls. Below each quote will be the date of the text and the English name of the modern book which contains the translation. For example, if the quote states *"Samurai and Ninja, 17th century"* it means that the translation of that document can be found in the book *Samurai and Ninja: The Real Story Behind the Japanese Warrior Myth that Shatters the Bushido Mystique* published by Tuttle in 2015. Each quote similarly has the English title of the book it can be found in for those who wish to read the original manuals themselves.

Finding Reliable Sources

As an author on the Special Forces of the middle ages I am often contacted by many people who tell me "I am a real spy" or "I work in security" or even "I am the last real ninja." Of course most, if not all, are extremely dubious. The research for this book has been myriad and extensive but above all it is different from my other works. Normally I focus on primary sources; however, for this project I have also had to delve into the subject of modern espionage. At the end of the book you will find a selected bibliography but I would like to point out that I have had the opportunity to talk to some people in the covert world and glean information from them on the parts of their work that are not public. I would like to reassure the reader that I have indeed ignored the clearly fake information that is out there. I have been as rigorous as I can in identifying people who really work in the covert industry and all the sub-branches. Rest assured that I am fully aware of the doubtful nature of most claimants. I truly hope that I have eliminated the false and brought about only a true representation of the modern world of covert operations, but any mistakes herein are mine and I hope they will be few or none at all.

A Warning about Ninja Masters

For those new to the world of the ninja and their history, be aware that in the second half of the 20th century and into the 21st century there are many people who claim or have claimed to be real ninja. They claim a lineage from older times and that they carry the secrets of the ninja. Many of these are Japanese and some of them are now deceased. The simple and stark fact is that there is not a single person or persons who has presented any realistic or reliable claim to being the inheritors of a real ninja tradition and none of them have ever produced any evidence to back up their claims. Therefore, when navigating the history of the ninja know that the arts of the ninja died out after the age of the samurai finished, and that while some people claim to be ninja and teach others the secrets of the ninja, there is no one on this planet who has ever produced a shred of evidence to support their claims. These assertions often do not match Japanese history and simply break down upon basic inspection.

Also, be very aware of anyone who claims or has ever claimed to teach a ninja hand-to-hand combat system known as ninjutsu, as this was an invention of the 20th century. While it is a positive thing to study and pass on ancient ninja ways, it must be done so from a historical basis and it is only through the study of the ancient scrolls left by real ninja that we can "carry the torch" of these arts to future generations.

While there is no one who can be found who has a living ninja tradition, there are people who do have a real connection to the ninja: 1) the sword school Katori Shinto-Ryu have a very small collection of warnings about ninja tactics in their oral tradition which form a guide on how to defend against ninja. These can be found in the back of the book *True Path of the Ninja* but must be observed with the understanding that oral tradition is the least reliable form of history; 2) Mr. Watanabe of Koka is a descendant of a real ninja and currently leads a very proactive society which preserves the history of the ninja; 3) the Ohara Family of Koka who descend from the Koka Koshi (ex-samurai of Koka) and who maintain their copy of the *Bansenshukai* manual; 4) Mr. Hagihara of Kyoto is the direct descendant of the *ronin* Hagihara Juzo of Mubyoshi-Ryu which produced the ninja scroll *Mizukagami* and he still holds the family scrolls; and finally, 5) the Yabutani and Natori families are the descendants of ninja in Wakayama—the Yabutani family are descended from the last grandmaster of Natori-Ryu which contains a system of ninjutsu, and the Natori family are the true descendants of Natori Sanjuro Masazumi, the author of the ninja manual *Shoninki*, the English translation of which is the main content of the above mentioned book *True Path of the Ninja*. These people are all descendants of ninja but do not carry a living tradition. They are simply descendants of people who were either ninja or those who wrote ninja scrolls.

Comparison not Continuation

The word *comparison* must be stressed here as this book will compare the principles and skills used by the shinobi of old and the members of today's special operations forces. It is not a continuation, meaning that the modern skills presented here are not skills passed down from the ninja of the past and which have been adapted for modern usage. They are two distinct sets of skills—those found in historical ninja manuals and those taught and used by today's agents. The aim of this book is to highlight the skill and ability of the ninja of old and show in comparison the realistic nature of their job, to wash away the fantasy image of the "super-ninja" and replace it with an understanding of the reality of these medieval commando-spies, while also allowing the community interested in the ninja to see inside the world of the modern covert agent. You will find that principles have remained the same but the skills change from period to period. There will be times when the content moves more into mainstream military tactics and times when they are not comparable, i.e., when modern inventions such as helicopters and electronic devices push the distance between them too far. Understand that this *comparison* of both principles and skills is an exercise in developing a respect for historical ninja and Japanese culture and to highlight the reality and true danger of modern espionage.

A Note on Terminology

In both military and samurai research there are a vast amounts of specific terminology used, sometimes technical, sometimes jargon, and sometimes slang. Furthermore, various military and paramilitary branches have their own variations of certain terms. Also, historically, different provinces, schools and eras in Japan used different sets of words. Therefore, it would be impossible in this book to conform to all variations and often it would make for a stagnant read. So I have opted to use terms that the public is more aware of in order that the text is accessible. But know that it is done so with the knowledge that it may sound unsuitable to a professional. I have kept the language as simple as possible and aimed at a vocabulary that a wider audience can connect with, avoiding jargon and messy terminology, as my aim is the education of the general public.

A Note on Technology

We live in an era where technology is progressing much faster than publication and therefore I have opted to omit any writings on covert technology. First of all, the speed in which it develops would render the information obsolete on publication. Within a few years of this book being available, it would very quickly become outdated and archaic. Also, the amount of research it would take to investigate modern cryptology, computer hacking and cyber espionage would be too vast a task for the parameters of this book; therefore, I have not included most discussions on technology. However, be aware that alongside the skills found in this book, there is a whole other world of cyber skills that continue to develop and grow and that those skills do play a parallel part in the world of the covert agent. Inside that world true specialists perform their important tasks daily.

Using the Word Shinobi Instead of Ninja

"Ninja" is a word commonly known in the English-speaking world. Both young and old will be able to tell you that the word ninja means a Japanese spy-commando or at least be able to identify it as a Japanese warrior or as a black-clad assassin. However, historical evidence shows that the word ninja was probably said as *shinobi no mono*. This is often contracted to simply *shinobi* but means the same thing. Also, the word *ninjutsu* was said as *shinobi no jutsu*, (skills of the ninja) and most connected root terms start with the base word, *shinobi* not *nin*. One of my principle aims is to change the use of the word ninja into the use of the word shinobi but as ninja is such a popular word, this is indeed a lifelong task. Therefore in this book I will use the word ninja with more frequency at the start but then towards the end focus on using the word *shinobi* and its derivatives so that you will hopefully use the word *shinobi* after you have finished reading this book.

Introduction:
The Shinobi and the Spy

*t*oday's spies, Special Forces members, paramilitary troops, security teams, kidnap and rescue groups and other such organizations are people who work in the covert world of espionage and special operations. In essence this means people who move behind enemy lines external to support from the main bulk of a military force, who operate either in enemy territory or close to the enemy and, therefore, danger. Furthermore, bodyguarding, personal protection and private investigation are also the tasks of modern agents. The ninja was a person or a unit of people hired to do a specific job inside the samurai army. They could have been from the samurai class all the way down to local thieves hired for covert operations, much in the same way that high-ranking officers run a covert force today while local guerrillas are used against an enemy. Likewise, spy masters were highest-ranking officials while at the lowest end were the street urchins, or beggars, collecting information for money. This means that spying and covert operations crossed all spectrums of society, but the main players were the upper classes, the officers and the samurai.

Irregular Warfare

While this book focuses on the ninja and a comparison to modern Special Forces and espionage agents, it often crosses into the boundaries of normal warfare. This is inevitable as ninja are very much a branch of the military machine. However, the ninja and today's special operatives both engaged in irregular warfare.

Allies use irregular warfare:

- To affect enemy morale
- To raise the morale of the allies
- To damage enemy materials and equipment
- To obtain enemy materials for allied use
- To damage communications
- To inflict damage on enemy personnel
- To improve allied communications
- To increase allied manpower
- To spy on the enemy through their communications
- To engage in propaganda
- To inflict maximum damage with minimal casualties
- To engage in covert destruction operations
- To aide in pre- and post-invasion

In war the enemy wish to:

- Indoctrinate
- Divide and rule
- Use allied material wealth
- Use allied manufacturing bases and workers
- Use allied communications
- Establish bases of power in allied lands
- Use allied personal as manpower

Both in modern times and in the ancient world, the above criteria have stood firm. It is only the landscape, the language, the people, the cultures and the technology that has changed. Throughout this book you will see that the ninja of old Japan performed all of the above and that they engaged in special operations to a level that is extremely professional. The ninja were an efficient tool in a warlord's army, the same as today's special operations agents.

Becoming a Ninja?

Each person studies an art for their own reasons. Some people wish to follow an ancient way; some simply like the aesthetics; while others wish to enrich themselves. There are those who only find that which is applicable to them today and there are those that simply practice costume play. None of these are negative as long as everybody gets what they want from following an ancient tradition. However, take care not to buy into the idea of "becoming a ninja."

The ninja existed in Japan between the 1300s and 1868. In order to become a ninja you would have to have trained in the arts of the ninja and be hired as a special forces agent or spy by a warlord. Unless you have the power to travel through time, you cannot actually become a ninja, much in the same way that you cannot become a Knight Templar or a Spartan warrior. Use the information in this book and our historical translations to obtain practical applications, to find a deeper meaning or to imagine the world of the ninja, taking a break from the mundane. But do not think you will be able to establish yourself as a ninja. Unfortunately those times have gone, but there is hope. You can always perfect your skills to the level of a real-life Japanese ninja, a goal that is within your grasp.

Skills Verses Principles

In essence, a principle does not change but a skill will transform. Sun Tzu listed five types of spies, a definition still accepted today. This is a principle. The skills of the spy will change from generation to generation, from coded messages carried by birds, to the most advanced communications technology today. Skills change while the principles remain the same. From ancient wrestling to modern cage fights, there are only a few locks that work on the human body. Infiltrating a castle in ancient China used the same principles as breaking into a compound in modern war-torn Africa. The principle remains the same while skills change. Take care to understand the difference between a skill that changes from time to time and a principle, a central theme that will never change in its essence.

Who Were the Ninja

The ninja was a military position in medieval Japanese armies. In Japanese the ninja was called *shinobi no mono* or sometimes shortened to just *shinobi*. It appears in the historical record between c.1375–c.1868. A Japanese army was made up of two main types of soldiers (plus conscripts). The first were *samurai*—the landed gentry-warrior. The second were the *ashigaru*—the professional and semi-professional foot soldiers. The ninja were from both of these classes; they could be a fully-fledged *samurai* or a foot soldier. The main point

SHINOBI NO MONO
INFILTRATOR

is that they were hired by a lord to perform the job known as *shinobi no mono* and they were put together in groups known as *shinobi-gumi and shinobi-shu*. This black ops team was attached to the army and worked in various roles. Some of them became sleeper agents among the enemy, some of them propaganda "merchants," while others were attached to the army as a special unit of commandos.

Consider these as medieval Japan's answer to the Navy Seals, the CIA, the SAS, MI5 and MI6. They were the dark operators of their time.

Know Your Ninja

The ninja and samurai research community—individuals and groups around the world who study the historical way of the ninja—employ English translations of old Japanese manuals on many subjects to investigate and navigate the world of ancient Japan. My team has published the widest range and the most translations of historical shinobi manuals from many historical writers; however, of all the ninja chroniclers, you should know the four pictured here.

HATTORI SENSEI
FROM MIKAWA
16TH CENTURY
SECRET TRADITIONS OF THE SHINOBI

ISSUI SENSEI
FROM KISHŪ
17TH CENTURY
TRUE PATH OF THE NINJA

FUJIBAYASHI SENSEI
FROM IGA
17TH CENTURY
THE BOOK OF NINJA

CHIKAMATSU SENSEI
FROM OWARI
17TH CENTURY
IGA AND KOKA NINJA SKILLS

Ninja or Thief?

The golden age of the ninja was around 1400–1600, the height of wartime medieval Japan. However, after the period of wars, samurai could find themselves without employment. Japanese armies were made up of up samurai retained to a lord but in times of war the lord hired *ronin* (masterless samurai) to add to their numbers. However, with no other prospects, many *ronin* became thieves.

The same is true of the ninja. Remember that the word *shinobi* means to infiltrate, so any thief also became known as shinobi. This has caused confusion because the military term *shinobi no mono* (a person who infiltrates) is a term for an army position. In time they become grouped with the shinobi considered to be thieves. As time passed, the social level of the ninja as a military position dropped to that of a night watchman and the myth of the low-level ninja thief began to emerge. Remember, a true ninja was not a thief. He was a special operations agent, but inevitably, people with such skillsets can sometimes turn to dark deeds and many outcast shinobi may have become thieves.

Understanding the Different Terms Used

Understanding the different Japanese terms can create problems but also, the difference between terms in the West can be an issue. Both the USA and the UK have different terms for their agents. In addition, different agencies use different terms. Plus, military forces and their various branches use their own particular jargon. To counter this I have put together a list below of the different terms and how they are used. Above all, I have opted for terms that will not create confusion for the general reader.

What are special forces?

Take care when thinking of the term Special Forces and consider them to be divided into two sections: 1) individuals who are a part of an army but who are well known for certain tasks, so that if a situation arises they are picked to undertake it; and 2) a group of people specially trained in certain areas such as infiltration, bomb

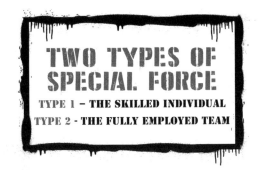

TWO TYPES OF SPECIAL FORCE

TYPE 1 – THE SKILLED INDIVIDUAL
TYPE 2 – THE FULLY EMPLOYED TEAM

disposal, surveillance, espionage, etc. The first are normally taken from a regular force when their skills are needed while the second are handpicked and formed into permanent or semi-permanent groups. This does not mean the second is better or more skilled. It normally means that the army is more structured with finances and can maintain specialized troops. With older armies in medieval times or less funded forces, specialized troops were often taken from the main force in times of need.

Examples of the first group are *eschelleurs*, skilled wall climbers, which in 1443 infiltrated and mapped out the city of Luxembourg as well as the commander of Duke Charles of Burgundy's bodyguard Olivier de la Marche, who was an expert in kidnapping. Such examples are people used for their skills when needed. Full-time modern Special Forces are an example of permanent troops. However, the shinobi of Japan actually fell into both categories. Shinobi could be either trained from within their family or inside the school (*ryu*) that they belonged to. This gave them systematic and defined training in a set of abilities as an individual but also, when an army was formed up from a conglomerate, normally a band of *shinobi* were also formed and men specialized in this task were used. These more often than not were called *Iga-shu* and *Koka-shu*—bands from the areas of Iga and Koka. These bands can, without question, be considered as falling under the title of Special Forces as their position and aim was almost exclusively used for clandestine operations. This means that shinobi are both type 1 and type 2 Special Forces—both individuals that are trained in clandestine skills who at times belong to a temporary troop and permanent sections with a specific role. Shinobi crossed the line between commando and spy and were used as single operators, spies and organized groups.

Organized army or independent warriors?

Special Forces tend to be units specially trained for a certain task but they remain a unit inside an organized force. However, in the medieval world, medieval armies tended to be a coalition of warriors, their armies held together by a collection of oaths, promises and political alignments which were only good for a limited period of time. This means that maintaining a specialized troop that only performed that role is difficult to identify. This means that while individuals in ancient times and the Middle Ages may have had abilities equal to or above Special Forces, they were abilities that were only useful when needed. Otherwise these individuals were simply a part of the army for the length of time the force held together. However, as time progressed, these individuals with exceptional skills who were called upon to perform deeds in times of need, grew and evolved into groups of specially trained units that were permanently employed in a military force, holding a very specific role. The level of skill may have been the same—the tasks they performed may have been the same—but the foundation of their identity and employment differed greatly.

Spy or commando?

The ninja are often thought of as spies but are most often reimagined in popular media as commandos. A spy is an agent positioned with the enemy or in contact with the enemy to gain information over a period of time. A commando uses clandestine operations in enemy territory to either gather information by observing the enemy while they are in hiding, or by taking covert action against the enemy. The problem here is that Japanese did not really separate the two. Some shinobi were purely spies and only ever acted as spies while others only ever acted as commandos; however, many shinobi would have had a foot in each camp, trained in both spying and commando skills. The result of this mixing of abilities was a true commando-spy. The classical Japanese word for a spy is *kanja*. It is probable that in earlier times, *kanja* meant spy and *shinobi* meant infiltrator, but afterwards these two terms became mixed.

PRIVATE INVESTIGATOR

TYPE 1: INVESTIGATORS WHO WORK WITHIN THE LAW

TYPE 2: THOSE WHO WORK OUTSIDE OF THE LAW

The information officer and the agent

The idea of what a ninja is lies in both our common understanding of spies and commandos; however, the world of spying uses a certain vocabulary that may differ slightly in different countries. On a basic level the spy can fall into two categories: the information officer and the agent.

High ability: Information officer (UK) and Agent (US)—These are highly-trained professional individuals in the arts of espionage who may or may not be public about what they do. Some are open about their work for the intelligence services while other will work covertly. This is the same in the world of the ninja. Open intelligence officers in ancient Japan were called *yo-nin*—"shinobi in the light" while covert officers were called *in-nin*—"shinobi in the dark." Covert officers may work in disguise as various professions or they may be in deep cover with different identities. The term "illegals" may be used for modern officers as they more often than not work in foreign lands and contrary to the laws of that nation. Furthermore, intelligence officers may at times run networks of "agents" or "informants."

Lower ability: Agents (UK) and Informant (US)—Also known as Covert Human Intelligence Sources (CHIS), these are individuals used for their social positions as information gatherers or informants. They may have some training and will be recruited by intelligence officers known as "handlers." In ancient Japan these individuals would be under the category of the *gokan* (five spies): local spies, internal spies, converted spies or doomed spies.

A problem arises when we look at the terminology used worldwide. For example, in the FBI or the CIA—American intelligence services—the term agent is used to identify a professional intelligence officer, while in the UK, the term intelligence officer is used to refer to this role. In the UK, a low-level individual who is recruited to feed information to the intelligence services because of their position in society is called an agent.

Special unit or single operator?

Another aspect to consider when thinking about Special Forces is the difference between Special Forces, spies, security teams and single operators. A Special Forces unit is a group of people; a spy is a person working in enemy territory either under cover or in obscurity; a security team is a private group; while a single operator is a lone person with a single mission or directive. The attraction of the iconic image of the ninja is that it represents all of these. While these tasks may not actually be performed by the same person, the term *shinobi* refers to an agent or agents that can work as a team, work alone under cover or move as a single operator behind enemy lines to perform clandestine operations. Make sure that you separate these roles and understand that *shinobi no mono* or ninja is a title and while a single ninja may be able to undertake all of these roles, the Japanese *shinobi* had specialists in all areas, meaning that there is no one single idea of what a ninja does, what they look like or what they can achieve. Remember *shinobi no mono* is an umbrella term to cover all.

Highly trained troops or special units?

Be careful not to mistake all highly trained or famous military units for Special Forces groups. Special Forces are mainly comprised of relatively small units that have specialized training in specific areas—demolition, infiltration, observation etc. There are also famous regular military units that have achieved fame

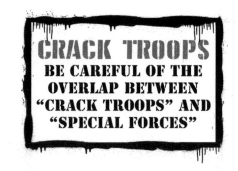

CRACK TROOPS
BE CAREFUL OF THE
OVERLAP BETWEEN
"CRACK TROOPS" AND
"SPECIAL FORCES"

for their quality in battle, such as the Persian Immortals, Spartans, Mameluks, Janissaries, English longbow men, Jagers and the German Stormtroopers of the First World War, all of which were well trained but are units considered to be "crack troops" *not* Special Forces.

What is a special operation?

A "special operation" is a mission and objective undertaken by a small group who, in a relatively short amount of time, bring about strategic and/or political change. It is normally undertaken by a force that is operating covertly or uses clandestine methods to achieve their goal. The financial and military input is usually vastly smaller and disproportionate to the results they achieve. They almost certainly undertake planned missions with specific goals and are not the results of good fortune in regular combat.

Types of special operations:

1. Destruction of infrastructure.
2. Destruction of weapon systems.
3. The targeting of people of importance for kidnapping, assassination or rescue.
4. The targeting of enemy of morale through attacking symbolic individuals, ideas, objects and places.

What is psychological warfare?

Psychological warfare is the act of attempting to change opinions of the masses, individual groups, specific members of society or of individuals. It is practiced in multiple ways but each action is undertaken specifically to change people's minds, normally to the detriment of the enemy. Examples of psychological warefare include swaying public opinion on political matters and targeting the ideology of certain groups or influential individuals. In old Japan this was done through the use of multiple shinobi agents spreading misinformation to the right people or by the use of various plots and schemes to separate allies by causing infighting between groups of enemy samurai. An example of then this would be useful is during a castle siege, when infighting might result in defenses falling thus allowing gaps in defensive lines to open.

What is espionage?

Espionage is the process of gathering nonpublic information in a secretive way. It is the realm of spies and is illegal and illicit in the country any agent is operating within. A charge of spying usually carrys severe punishment including death. It is also the realm of influence, with operatives working to plant false information and work against enemy spies. Espionage operations have a central hub and teams of agents, either working alone or in separate teams and in separate locations. Both agents and teams feed information back to a central hub where the information is scrutinized for accuracy and authenticity which is then used to build a picture of the enemy and is used alongside "open information gathering."

In Japan, a classic spy was known as *kanja* which means: "a person who uses gaps," literally "gap-person," whereas *shinobi no mono* were infiltrators mostly used in commando-style operations. However, as previously stated, both terms and skill sets appear to have been mixed in later Japan and are used interchangeably.

What is surveillance?

Surveillance is the task of "watching" a target's movements, activities and thoughts for prolonged periods of time in order to develop a psychological profile. In ancient times this was an integral part of shinobi activities. Today, this can be divided into two areas:

Directed surveillance—External viewing, or following a target and mapping their routine. This is performed in order to obtain detailed accounts of a target's movements by observing them from a covert position.

Intrusive surveillance—Planting listening devices and to observe the "internals" of the target's life resulting in being on the inside of their personal environment without them being aware of the intrusion.

What are clandestine operations?

The words clandestine and espionage are often used together and they are similar. However, clandestine means to be kept secret, unknown and illicit, while espionage means to learn secrets about other people. Espionage may be clandestine in nature, however, in popular media, clandestine operations often refer to the operations of "special forces" and "black ops" groups. In this book, when I refer to clandestine operations, I will be mainly referring to commando-like raids and covert operations. However, be aware of the difference between clandestine and espionage.

What is open information gathering?

Open information gathering is the collection of publicly available information, from media sites and public government files to trade and tax information. A vast amount of information can be gathered on a target area through open information and a detailed profile of a person or target area and country can be obtained by channeling all of that information into a cohesive structure. Open information gathering was the primary aim and most time-consuming practice of the historical shinobi. Ninja would have spent a vast amount of their time wandering the lands of the enemy, talking to the people, observing the highways and byways and mapping out each area, its urban planning and fortifications while simultaneously recording the wealth, number, morale and customs of its people.

What is terrorism and freedom fighting?

Terrorism is violent action (mainly employed by small groups) which pushes a political agenda and a change to government policy through external pressure in order to force ideals or wishes upon others. They hold the aim of overthrowing a ruling power. On the other hand, "freedom fighters" are groups that wish to overthrow overtly aggressive or corrupt governments and wish to establish a more peaceful regime that offers their people more liberty. However, a ruling class will always identify groups who use violence to achieve their aims as terrorists, while these same groups will always identify themselves as freedom fighters. The actual difference between the two groups is based on opinion and political viewpoint.

What is cyber espionage?

Cyber espionage is the gathering of information from digital networks such as the Internet, company networks and all networks where digital information is shared. Hostile individuals, in this case "hackers," can "mine" all of these networks, often from a remote position, where they can gain vast amounts of information. What is commonly known as "hacking" can also be known as Computer Network Exploitation (CNE). Outside of other governments that perform cyber espionage, there are also independent activist groups known as "hacktivists," each with their own agenda.

What is propaganda?

Propaganda is the use of information in all its forms to present a misleading and skewed version of an idea, event or objective. Often the information is biased and misleading in the hope that people will be influenced unreasonably and that the continuation of propaganda will gain support or objections to a certain cause. This is either done to the enemy, or internally, the latter being so that a government's own people maintain order. This is also common in the world of advertising where, even within the limitations of strict guidelines, information is presented in a way to lead a customer to buy an item they may not actually want or have never desired. Propaganda is used to change the hearts and minds of others by devious means.

The Spiritual Quest

The ways of the samurai and shinobi are the ways of the military. A common trap to avoid is to perceive the ways of the samurai and shinobi as spiritual enlightenment. The seeds of this trait appear as a small sapling, and over many years, if not centuries, this has now grown into a full blown oak tree of misunderstanding.

People often come to the Japanese martial arts in the pursuit of something spiritual, a way to redefine their understanding of universal human questions and to walk a path that will lead them to become better people. Their intention is pure, but they often mistake the ways of the samurai and shinobi as the way of peace and of Zen. In truth, the samurai and Zen Buddhism have a long and complex relationship and are indeed interconnected; however, originally there was a distinction between military skills and a spiritual path. Samurai waged war in a practical sense, to help them defeat and kill others; however, they would also incorporate religious philosophies into their practice, including Buddhism, Shinto, Confucianism and some Taoism, each one moving in and out of favor as Japanese society progressed. The samurai did not enter a military path to achieve enlightenment, rather they did it because it was their business to know how to kill. Of course, as a medieval society, religion and war combined to a high level and the samurai held beliefs in magic spells, sacred chants and deep esoteric doctrines, but they did not engage with military ways to find a path of self-perfection.

Later on, as time passed, the samurai were all but redundant in Japanese society and many found themselves with a steady livelihood, but with minimal purpose. And like all warriors in times of peace, they sought for something more. It was then that the ways of the samurai became more spiritual. It was in times of peace, in the post-samurai era, that we see a move towards the "do" arts, *iaido*, *kyudo* and later *aikido* and *karatedo*, where a heavy influence of Zen is present. The 20th century brought these spiritual ways to the West, and Western people were greatly attracted to this deep and fulfilling path. Often Westerners would pursue the "do" arts to perfect character. As ninjutsu was mistakenly seen as a hand-to-hand martial art in the second half of the 20th century, a craze of spiritual ninja awareness arose alongside it.

The spiritual should not be mistaken for discipline. It is absolutely correct to seek out discipline and right attitude in the ways of the historical samurai of Japan, but it is not correct to look for religious instruction in military study. To better understand this, imagine an American soldier who joined the army to follow and better understand Christianity and the concept of enlightenment. It would simply not seem logical. That same soldier would actually have joined the service to understand the ways of war and to develop discipline in their life. In the process, they would serve their country but they would engage with a preacher or army chaplain to worship their God. There is no doubt that religion and war go hand in hand, even in today's modern society, but a person who wishes to pursue military ways, discipline and spirituality has one foot in the armed forces and the other in religion or a philosophical system. Likewise, a samurai was born into a military family or was a warrior who was embroiled in an age of wars. They too would have entered a military school to learn the ways of conflict. They would have been associated with various religious sects as they also had a need to understand both the world around them and to navigate the treacherous waters of the stress caused by killing. To truly replicate the ways of the samurai, it is best to divide the realm of practical military study and of religion, but know that they are indeed linked. However, they cannot be fully interchangeable.

Reconstructing the Way We Think

Dividing the military from the spiritual while leaving an overlapping link between them must bring about a new way of thinking. Instead of entering into the study of the shinobi with the idea of enlightenment, step into the study with the aim of perfecting military skills as a branch of samurai warfare. On the other hand, you may bolster your training with your preferred religious teachings or philosophical ways. This will run alongside your study of combat and tactical methods. And it does not have to be Japanese. There were hundreds of thousands of Christians in Japan during the height of the shinobi and some samurai and lords opted to follow Christianity, which in the end got them killed or expelled when the religion was banned. Use the following list to structure your training:

- Study a school of war (*gungaku*)
- Study a school of combat (projectiles, blades, polearms, hand to hand, etc.)
- Study a school of shinobi arts
- Investigate religion and religious philosophy
- Investigate the occult and magic

The Ninja Myth

The ninja have undergone many transformations (see Stephen Turnbull's book *Ninja: Unmasking the Myth*) and each generation has reinvented the ninja for their own reasons.

The author Antony Cummins with Stephen Turnbull in Japan, both researching the historical ninja.

Readers may remember the 1960s ninja. At that time, in the West, the ninja was thought of as a magical black wizard or black-clad thief. He was famously depicted as the enemy of James Bond. In the 1970s and 1980s he was imagined as a hand-to-hand combat expert, metal chains and throwing stars slashing out at the screen. The 1990s and early 2000s saw the evolution of the ninja as a warrior on a spiritual quest, a peace bringer and calmer of the mind using a mysterious philosophy. Finally, today we are starting to see the historical ninja appear as a true-to-life representation of the past.

CHAPTER 1

THE SECURITY TEAM AND SHINOBI SQUAD

*T*here are different terms used for covert teams, such as Paramilitary Unit (colloquial), Private Military Unit (colloquial) and Risk Management Team but here we shall refer to them as the "security team." These terms may refer to nonmilitary teams—which means they are not an official squad working for a nation's military—however they will normally be filled with ex-military personnel or current military personnel who are working "off the books." The professionalism and ability will vary from team to team.

Members of a Security Team

The following are members of a "standard" security team or at least the broad definitions between the different teams around the world. A security team is a collection of people who work in the private sector who normally have some form of special training and who travel the world, moving in and out of warzones, being paid to perform military tasks but without being attached to the military. This can involve assassination/murder, kidnap and rescue, destruction of technology (such as a downed aircraft in enemy territory), the burning of opponent drug stores (i.e., one drug lord attacking another drug lord) and many other similar activities. Sometimes they are commissioned by the military (and some of them are full military teams who do this in their "spare time") but often it is normal and wealthy individuals who pay well to get a job finished who are not constrained by the rules of war. The term also applies to people who perform security for high-risk companies. The list below outlines some specialist members of a military team outside of the "standard" operative.

Long eye

The sniper of the team, a member who deals with longer range weapons and who will cover the team from a distance.

Trunk monkey

When in a larger vehicle, there is normally some form of heavy weapon mounted or ready to use. This can even be mounted in the open on the back of jeeps, the operator of this is affectionately known as a "trunk monkey."

Cyber specialist

A person who deals with the online and technical element of the team's needs, from computer technology to online investigation. This is a role that is extremely specialized.

Local national

A local national is a person who is a native to that country and who has connections in the "underworld," organized crime and the military. They are used to facilitate a smooth insert into the area and to create connections and organize meets. They act as guides and as the team's connection to local customs, problems and situations. They bring about meetings with the correct people, such as those crime lords or warlords who control the area. Without them a situation can become complex and difficult. They sometimes act as combatants.

Members of a Shinobi Squad

Historically the Japanese use terms like "-*gumi*" or "-*shu*" to mean team or squad. For example, "*shinobi-gumi*" which means ninja squad, or *Iga-shu* and *Koka-shu* which means the group from Iga and the group from Koka—both of which were famous for shinobi and became bywords for "ninja team." The following breakdown of a ninja team comes from *The Book of Ninja* (1676).

Shite 仕手—The main infiltrator

Pronounced *she-te*, highly skilled in the arts of burglary *and* infiltration including tools, works deep inside the enemy house and carries out the main objective of the mission.

Shitezoe 仕手添—Supporters to the main infiltrator

Infiltrates alongside the main performer but branches off to report on the status of the enemy inside.

Tsuronin 通路人—Liaison

Moves between the *shitezoe*, deep inside the enemy complex and the agents outside, transporting messages between the internal and external members.

Aizu mocha 相圖持—Signal senders

Communications, they use sound and a visual signals, both of which are used to convey prearranged ideas.

Hari 張—Watchmen

Lesser-skilled agents who take up position at specified locations and who observe and raise the alarm if an enemy advances into their position.

This is the end of the list from *The Book of Ninja*. The above members are mainly used on missions of infiltration and breeching a compound. Other detailed examples of ninja teams can be found in *Iga and Koka Ninja Skills*.

Kyodo—Local guides

The ninja scroll shoninki explains local guides, people who are often low level whose main attribute is that they know the local area and can steer a team in a way that strangers to the area cannot.

PRIMARY EVIDENCE

Kyodo: this refers to when you don't know about the enemy's district. It is the art of building a rapport with local inhabitants, be aware that even an idiot living in that region would be more helpful than outsiders who insist that they know the place very well. Thus, it is said you should ask a local inhabitant for anything when you are in an unfamiliar area.

—*True Path of the Ninja* (1681)

Kanja

A *kanja* is a classic spy, someone who walks among the enemy or in fact lives with them. The roles of the *kanja* are varied. Sometimes the word *kanja* and *shinobi no mono* are interchangeable; however, when looked at in detail, *kanja* always represents a classic spy. These can be spies planted in enemy territory and can be used as a modern security team uses local nationals to act as a liaison between people in that area or put shinobi in contact with the correct people. The difference between *kyodo* (local guides) and *kanja* (spies) is that a local guide simply has

KANJA
SHINOBI INFILTRATOR

knowledge of the area. It is the place where they live, whereas a *kanja* is a person in the area who works in the espionage world, as a local national would.

PRIMARY EVIDENCE

Kanja use intermediaries to gather information or at times make themselves as intermediaries.

—*The Book of Samurai* series (17th century)

If the local agent in your plan is not good enough or is inexperienced, you should make yourself a servant to him and enter the enemy castle with them. You should have made arrangements with your lord for the signals needed and set fire at the most appropriate time.

—*The Book of Ninja* (1676)

Equipment

Equipment will often not be standard as they are with regular military units. The following is a selected list of equipment from the *Special Operations Executive Manual* in World War II:

- Flares
- Fuses and timers
- Grenades
- Limpet devices (bombs that stick to things)
- Wire cutters
- Crowbars
- Knives
- Grapples
- Medical kit
- Rations
- Poison capsules
- Secret inks
- Amphibious breathing equipment
- Ladders and climbing equipment

Shinobi equipment is strikingly similar, the following list is compiled from various historical manuals:

- Flares
- Torches and lights
- Fuses and timers
- Grenades
- Wire cutters
- Crowbars
- Knives
- Grapples
- Medical kit
- Rations
- Poison
- Secret inks
- Amphibious breathing equipment

- Ladders and climbing equipment

Equipment varies depending on the task—demolition will need explosives, castle infiltration will need long ladders and house burglary will need breaking and entering tools. Therefore, each situation requires different tools for the job.

CHAPTER 2

CORE SKILLS

*t*he arts of the shinobi are an auxiliary art—they are added to a person's core skill set. A member of a Special Forces team would not become a member without such skills, a cyber-spy would not be in high-end security without them and a ninja would not be a ninja without needed skills that were found outside of ninjutsu. Often the question arises as to what does, and what does not, constitute a shinobi skill—what is *shinobi no jutsu* and what is not *shinobi no jutsu*? There is a blurred line between them, an area where it is difficult to define if something is or is not ninjutsu. However, there are definite sides to that area—there are skills that do come under the umbrella term of ninjutsu and there are skills that do not. This chapter will look at those skills needed as a foundation for life as a shinobi; they are skills that are not considered as shinobi arts but are skills that are shared by most warriors. Long distance travel was used by messengers, weapon usage and hand-to-hand combat was a staple of warrior training and arresting skills were used by anyone given the task of making an arrest. These skills are not considered as ninjutsu, but they are fundamental for warriors. In early Japan the family would teach its warriors their secret fighting arts, and later schools formed with their own syllabi. It was after or alongside these core sections that the way of the shinobi was taught. Agents must have a basic skill set to rest their abilities on.

Physical Fitness

Physical fitness is just a *must* in Special Forces but may be less of a requirement for classic spies (in some cases). To travel extreme distances, climb mountains and cross rivers in all weather, you have to be physically fit. However, do not mistake "muscle bound" for fitness. Both those who are overweight and those who weigh a lot due to heavy lifting are not much use in the field, because if they get shot and wounded, teammates will need to carry them. Therefore, stamina is more important than strength—endurance is the key in all matters. Long distance walking, running, mountain climbing and swimming in all conditions is the best form of training. It is important to maintain a good level of fitness and dexterity.

Long Distance Travelling

An agent has to be able to perform long distance travel, over all sorts of terrain and through enemy land. The ways of the shinobi and modern agent may be discussed and trained for in the gym or dojo, but the reality of the training is found in the mountains, forests, the deserts and urban areas. You can't be fully prepared by simply traning within the confines of a dojo. After studying inside, move outside and get into the wilderness.

The following elements are required for long distance travel:
- Mapping out multiple routes
- Identifying checkpoint positions
- Identifying dangerous areas controlled by the enemy
- Deciding where to use main routes
- Deciding whether or not to travel off road and through harsh areas
- Navigation in day and night (including star maps)

- Moving from water source to water source
- Establishing meeting points for contacts
- Establishing observation points (OPs)
- Signals and communication
- Staying out of sight
- Sleeping in the wilderness
- Escape routes
- Drop points (if possible)
- Equipment dumps

Above all, shinobi and modern agents need to be able to move at speed—move light—either stealing equipment and rations along the way or being able to live off the land until a destination is reached, something which is done in enemy territory.

Weapons

You should understand the difference between a weapon, an improvised weapon and a tool. A weapon is designed to kill or maim, a tool has a practical function, and an improvised weapon is an object not normally used in violence which is used violently. A sword is made to kill and a hammer is made to hammer nails, but a hammer can also be used to kill. The samurai used a large variety of weapons, from the short daggers to long pikes, from thrown blades to large projectiles. They studied the arts of fire and explosives and used animals to their advantage. However, even with such a large array of weapons at their command, most people only see the samurai as a swordsman. The truth is that samurai were primarily mounted horse archers, and their entire ethos revolved around the bow. It was much later that the spear and then the sword became central to their identity. Such common misconceptions often skew our understanding of old Japan—the case is even more drastic with the ninja. Forget ninja stars and ninja claws. They are a 20th century myth. Historical ninja tools and weapons which are found in the records clearly divide between weapons and tools.

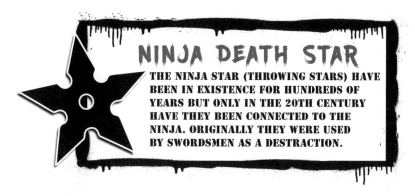

NINJA DEATH STAR

THE NINJA STAR (THROWING STARS) HAVE BEEN IN EXISTENCE FOR HUNDREDS OF YEARS BUT ONLY IN THE 20TH CENTURY HAVE THEY BEEN CONNECTED TO THE NINJA. ORIGINALLY THEY WERE USED BY SWORDSMEN AS A DESTRACTION.

There are very few "ninja weapons" just as there are very few knives that only cooks use. The shape and size tend to be useful for most people. Therefore, shinobi used the same weapons the samurai used as they were samurai, foot soldiers or bandits hired to perform the role for a short period. However, shinobi picked the most convenient weapons for the task at hand and they travelled lightly. Ninja tools on the other hand are a different matter. Most "ninja tools" are just normal tools used for a stealthy purpose, such as the grappling hook. Such hooks were used in a wide range of occupations in Japan, but when used by a person to climb a wall at night, to infiltrate an enemy camp, an innocent tool became a "shinobi tool." Likewise, a nail extractor used by builders becomes a shinobi tool when used on a mission, as does a drill, saw, torch, crow bar etc. There are only a handful of items that can be said to be "shinobi tools." These include sleeping powders, low-light torches, extendable saws, etc.—tools which are specifically used for breaking and entering. In addition to this, the shinobi had a great understanding how fire could be used from a military standpoint and it is here where *shinobi no jutsu*—the arts of the ninja and *kajutsu*—and the art of fire cross over.

KAJUTSU
THE ART OF FIRE

SHINOBI NO JUTSU
THE ARTS OF THE SHINOBI

Do not imagine the *shinobi* as a black clad figure with shuriken in hand and straight blade on the back. Instead picture a samurai captain on a military campaign, with a selection of tools suited for each mission, and a team of highly skilled warriors with him, all trained in the arts of the ninja, masters of fire, explosives, murder and espionage. All of them are attached to the main army and all of them physically fit and who as a team travel before the main force or infiltrate the enemy at night.

The following sections will look at the various weapons and their parts and uses. The main point to keep in mind for both old Japan and the modern world is that weapons tended to be the same across all forces but with slight difference in use. Some people shoot a pistol close to their face and move in a snake like manner around corners, others keep their weapon close to the chest, and only bring it out when the first shot has been fired. Even in the late 1500s to the first half of the 1600s, samurai like Miyamoto Musashi complained that other samurai did not fight correctly, or that a specific style was not used correctly. This rivalry between styles seems to be common worldwide and in all aspects of life—in sports, teams all play the same sport but often fans of different teams believe that their rivals do not use their skills correctly and in today's traditional samurai schools, many members of one school believe that other samurai schools practice incorrectly—the cycle goes on. In the following sections, I will present weapon typology, parts and some basic uses. But remember that above all, weapons training is practiced in the basic stages of military training and as a person becomes more specialized, they learn to manipulate weapons to a higher level and in different ways. However, even with these skills in place, the old shinobi and modern security team value surprise and horrific tactics to ensure victory over a fair fight.

Range

Each weapon has its own range of distance for engagement. This starts at the furthest distance and moves to the shortest. Most action is done with small arms,

GENERAL COMPARISON

LONG RANGE		
PRIMARY		
SIDE ARM		
RESERVE		
GRAPPLING		

A comparison of weapons used by standard military in both samurai times and today. Their positions can change depending on the period of samurai warfare.

the primary weapons of a security team member, normally used within the visual range of a person. Longer distances are for sniping and shorter distances are for close and unarmed combat. In old Japan, the bow was the primary weapon but by the 1500s it had been replaced by the spear and sword. The difference between the modern warrior and the samurai is that the primary weapons of the samurai were for the most part bladed, but today, the rifle or small arms have become the primary weapons. Therefore, a samurai would have used bows and projectiles for long distance, a sword or spear for up close and side arms and knives when in hand-to-hand combat. In range order, weapons fall into the categories of long, primary, sidearm, reserve and unarmed.

When a warrior takes up the role of shinobi his focus on weapons changes and moves down a size category.

OVERALL COMPARISON

	MODERN	STANDARD SAMURAI	SHINOBI
PRIMARY			
SIDE ARM			
RESERVE			

A comparison of the primary, sidearm and reserve weapons of modern special operations, standard samurai and shinobi.

Parts of a gun

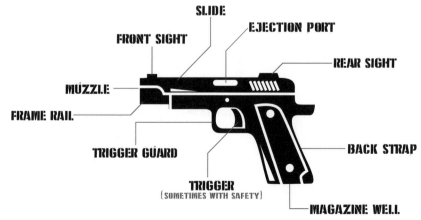

Overt carry

An overt carry of a weapon is a weapon holstered in full view of the public. Law enforcement officers and military personal overtly carry weapons, just as samurai carried their swords in an overt manner.

Covert carry

A covert carry it to carry a weapon where people cannot see it, such as in the front of a belt, under clothing, or holstered at the side covered by a jacket. Covert carry affects the way that the weapon is drawn. Samurai also carried covertly in the form of a blade known as the *shinobi-zashi*—hidden sidearm. The use of the word shinobi here does not mean ninja; it means hidden in stealth or to be hidden.

The suppressor

Everyone knows the movie trope of the silenced gun that uses an attachment called a "silencer." However, it is more correct to use the term "*suppressor*." It is not that the word "silencer" is not used, but security teams tend to use the word suppressor because the tool does not render a shot silent; it simply reduces the amount of noise, but it can still be heard. In addition to this is the *flash suppressor* helps remove flash from a gun's muzzle.

The three sounds of a gun

A gun actually makes noise in three ways:

1. Mechanical—the noise of the gun internals moving.
2. Muzzle—the noise of the gas exiting the muzzle.
3. Bullet—the sound or crack of a bullet that breaks the sound barrier.

The shinobi recorded a recipe for silent gunpowder to try to help eliminate sound. This is found in the shinobi tools section of the Bansenshukai manual.

PRIMARY EVIDENCE

ナラズ薬
Silent Gunpowder

- Saltpeter: 100 Momme* (This should be roasted down to about 70 Momme)
- Sulphur: 11 Momme (cover large chunks of sulphur with and rice paste, expose to rain or dew for one hundred days and nights)
- Ash: 8 Momme
- Uchi: 3 Momme 5 Bu
- Charred tiger fur: 3 Momme
- Charred droppings of the cormorant bird: 1 Momme
- Broiled bones of a Sea Bream
  —*The Book of Ninja* (1676)

*A momme is a unit of weight equal to 3.75 grams.

Swords

Swords are emblematic of the warrior and have become a staple of the idea of warrior culture, even though many warriors in history used other weapons. In Japan, there were multiple types of swords:

1. Ceremonial great-sword (細太刀) *hosodachi.*
2. Practical great-sword (野太刀) *nodachi.*
3. Great-sword (太刀) *tachi.*
4. Standard term for sword (刀) *katana.*
5. Practical striking swords (打刀) *uchigatana.*
6. Greater sidearm (大脇差) *owakizashi.*
7. Sidearm (脇差) *wakizashi.*
8. Hidden sidearm (忍指) *shinobi-zashi.*
9. Head-taking dagger (首切り刀) *kubikirigatana.*
10. Armor-piercing dagger (鎧通) *yoroidoshi.*

This list gives the basic range of Japanese swords and while more variations exist, these ten constitute the main swords used by the samurai.

Parts of a sword

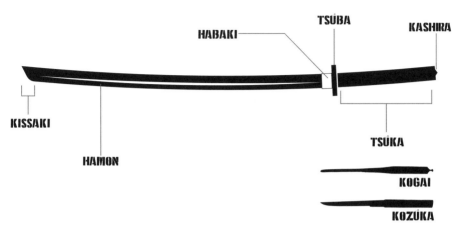

The parts of a Japanese sword are numerous and the subject goes deep.

Weapon Use: Primary Weapon

The primary weapon today is the rifle, the side arm is the pistol and the reserve is a dagger. For the conventional samurai, the primary weapon would be the bow or the spear, the side arm the sword and the reserve weapon the dagger. However, this book is focusing on shinobi and Special Forces in old Japan which means that the primary weapon for shinobi would in fact be a sword, the side arm would be the short sword and the reserve weapon would be the dagger; however, the type of mission dictated what weapons the shinobi used—they may have only taken a side arm with them if the situation demanded it or they may have opted for simply a dagger. Historical records show that at times shinobi stashed their main weapons and armor before they burgled a house. The following sections assume that you know how to use a weapon in the standard way and will outline basic safety and some elements of use outside that of basic postures and positions of fire and use.

Rifle hands

Whenever you are practicing movement and rifle tactics, but do not have a rifle or a dummy rifle, place your hands in the fashion shown in the illustration. Avoid using the version of the finger on

the trigger and opposite hand upturned like you would in a child's game. Hold the hands flat and aim at the intended target.

Check to the rear

An actual life threatening situation where life is truly in danger produces "tunnel vision" which leads a person to focus only to the front and not to the environment around them. Therefore, in practice, every shot or burst of shots should be followed by checking the environment to the left rear and then to the right rear, returning the head to a forward position to check your weapon and then be ready for the next exercise or engagement. Practicing this will enforce the ritual of checking all areas, even at the height of danger.

CHECK YOUR SURROUNDINGS
- CHECK LEFT REAR
- CHECK RIGHT REAR
- FACE FORWARD

Muzzle discipline

Muzzle discipline is the ability to maintain control of where your gun muzzle is at all times—whether you are actively shooting, at rest or standing and walking with your gun drawn.

In practice—From the lowest level to the highest ability, muzzle discipline should be conformed to—team safety is paramount. No matter if it is a replica training weapon or a fully-loaded live weapon, never point it at a person or allow your line of fire to be in line with a team member or training partner when holding a weapon. When it is agreed that training has begun, the muzzles of practice weapons should only be aimed at a training partner for the short time that a certain skill is being practiced. In between practice, the muzzle should be pointed downwards.

Examples of good (below) and bad (above) muzzle discipline.

In action—When in battle or in a live fire exercise, muzzles are of course pointed forward; however when a team member needs to cross your field of view or when you need to turn and move past a person, the muzzle of the weapon should be dipped. Practice turning and allowing people to cross your line of fire by dipping the weapon in a fluid motion and then bringing it back up. Train this until it is second nature. Also, after you have fired a weapon at a target, drop the muzzle and angle it downwards to get used to returning it to this position.

There is a live fire exercise where two teammates will stand at opposite ends of the range with a target next to each of them. This exercise is allows a person to become used to shots being fired past or around them. However, safety should be maintained at all times.

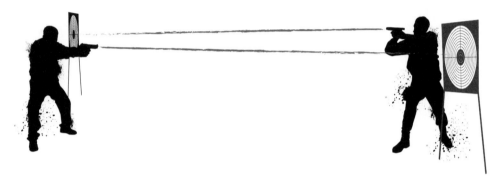

Safety with a Japanese sword

As with guns, a sword's purpose is to kill. Safety should be used and caution taken when around other people. The following instructions will help avoid accidental injury.

Carry the sword with the thumb over the hilt—Always put your thumb over the hilt when you hold a sword. This stops the sword from sliding out of its scabbard or prevents people from taking it.

UDENUKI

SAGEO

Check the peg—Make sure that the peg in the sword's hilt is tight in its slot. If it falls out when you are using the sword the blade may come out, or worse, fly out when you cut. It is proper for a samurai sword to have two pegs.

Taking the sword out of the scabbard—When you wish to take a sword out to look at it or show it to someone, hold it horizontally and blade up. Place one hand on the scabbard, palm upwards, while the other hand grips the handle. Gently "break" the seal of the sword in the scabbard and then softly push the back of the blade down onto the scabbard and draw it out horizontally so that the blade edge does not touch the wood inside. The sword is returned to the scabbard in the same way.

Pass the sword with the blade toward you—Whenever you pass a blade to someone, turn it so that the blade edge is facing you and you have a controlled grip on the handle. Then, pass it to the other person, ensuring that they are grasping the handle. Gently let go when you are sure they have control. They should pass it back in the same manner.

Quick Skills

The following small selection of skills are simple tricks to add to any basic training that you have had in weapon usage. These are used to help you in specific situations where you may be in trouble.

Magazine dumping

To "dump" a magazine is to fire a full magazine of rounds at the enemy in one continuous burst. When contact is made with an enemy and they gain an advantage over the security team, the team is then "behind the curve" or "one beat" or "one step" behind the enemy. To rectify this, one member of the security team will empty a full magazine in the direction of the enemy contacts without much thought on accuracy. The intention is simply to put the enemy "on the back foot" and for the security team to get "ahead of the curve." At this point, other members of the team will use this change in rhythm to place accurate shots on the enemy which allows the team to take control of the situation and results in the enemy being "one step behind."

Harassing fire

Harassing fire is similar to the above "magazine dumping" but with more control. In this situation, the security team fires more rounds with less accuracy at the enemy to force them to move or stop firing. This forces an enemy onto the back foot and allows the team to engage their tactics. Magazine dumping is an emergency tactic in a very tight situation while harassing fire is used to take control of a situation when both teams are equal.

Quick-sniper

The quick sniper is an *ad hoc* skill used when time is short or when a nonprofessional shooter is performing a shot outside the normal range. The skill is to lie down at a 90 degree angle to the muzzle, with the rifle resting on your non-trigger forearm, your arms positioned as if cradling a baby. Before settling into position, remove one boot and sock, fill the sock with sand, gravel or soil and tie the top. This forms a type of "beanbag." Adopt the position shown below and hold the filled sock with your non-trigger hand, resting the elbow of the trigger hand on it. This forms a wide triangle base for you to steady the shot. You then squeeze or release your grip on the filled sock to alter the vertical angle of the muzzle—when squeezed the muzzle will be pushed down, when you relax your grip the gun stock will drop and the muzzle will rise naturally. Use the correct pressure on the filled sock to aim at the target, breath slowly, then breathe out and take the shot. This skill is only used as an emergency when a proper set up is not available.

The cradle

In both modern times and in old Japan people would use a cradle to make a steady shot. Suspend the rifle on a rope or something similar as shown and use this as a steady firing platform. Today, cradles are often used when firing from helicopters.

Modern cradles are used in the same manner as they were in old Japan. Today they are often used in vehicles.

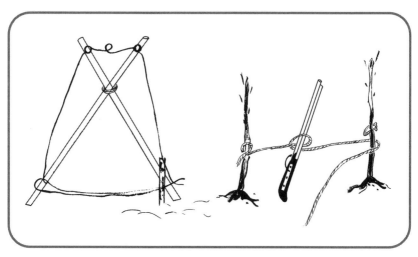

A military scroll kept in the National Archives of Japan showing
the use of the cradle in samurai shooting.

Weapon Use: Sidearm

The sidearm is the first weapon reached for if the primary weapon fails or if the
distance too short. For the modern warrior this is a pistol—for the warrior of old
Japan this was a *wakizashi*. Issui-sensei of Natori-Ryu in his ninja scroll *True Path
of the Ninja* states that a shinobi should only use a sidearm when infiltrating (most
likely because longer weapons are cumbersome); however, other shinobi masters
such as Fujibayashi-sensei actually use the term *tachi* meaning "great sword." The
following is a selection of uses for the sidearm.

SINGLE OPERATOR COMPARISON

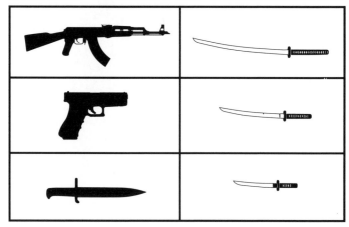

The gun grip

The way of holding the pistol is of great importance and can drastically improve shooting prowess. The pistol should be held in an isometric pressure grip and not in the "T-cupping" form.

Isometric pressure grip—The isometric pressure grip forms a strong triangle, giving the shot a stable base. Pull the non-trigger hand backwards against the lower three fingers of the trigger hand by using the hips and shoulders to form a strong and harmonious connection. The trigger is gently squeezed and rounds are fired.

The "T-cupping" grip—This grip is a bad habit and should not be used. When the gun fires, this style allows it to jump upwards out of the hand and does not allow for a strong platform.

Sword grips

When gripping a Japanese sword there are two basic concerns—whether to grip with a single hand or with two hands and relaxing certain fingers. The famous swordsman Miyamoto Musashi states that a Japanese sword must only ever be held in one hand unless extra power is needed; however, other schools employ the method of holding with two hands. Multiple accounts show that the sword should be held with the thumb and index finger relaxed and the three lower fingers tight.

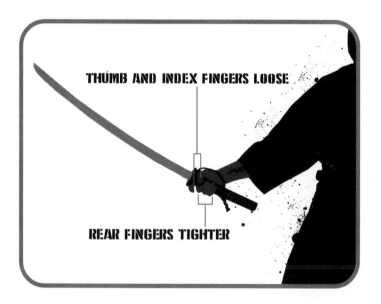

PRIMARY EVIDENCE

To grasp the sword, give your thumb and index finger a sense of floating, keep your middle finger neither tight nor loose and tighten your ring and little finger.
—Miyamoto Musashi, *The Book of Five Rings* (c.1645)

When striking with the sword, keep the inside of the hand relaxed, hold the hilt tightly with the rear fingers, push slightly forward and then cut by pulling. Hold your breath on the strike.
—*The Book of Samurai Series* (17th century)

Positioning of the non-shooting hand

In all sidearm draws, the non-shooting hand is placed on the body out of the way—in almost all cases, this is on the chest. The reason for this is that when drawing a weapon people tend to shoot before the second hand has connected with the gun. This can result in people shooting off their own fingers. The correct procedure is to draw and shoot at the hip while at the same time placing the non-shooting hand on the chest, after the first shot, bring the gun forward and place the non-shooting hand in the isometric pressure grip (see p. 49) and then fire again. In all situations when firing with a single hand, the opposite hand should be placed out of the way on the body.

Types of sidearm draws

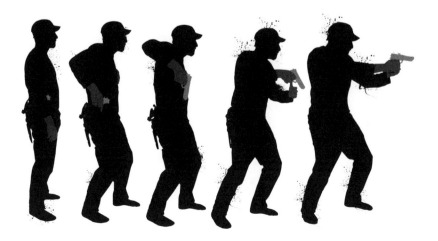

The standard hip draw—A fluid draw from the hip, the image on the previous page has been slightly exaggerated to show the movement; however, compact and quick action is needed.

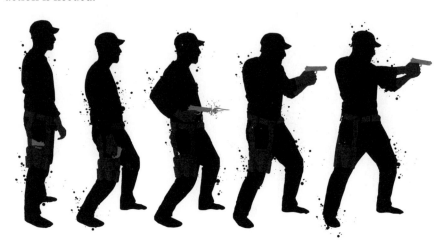

The thigh rig—When drawing from a thigh rig, there is a tendency to lean to one side to draw the weapon which creates imbalance. This is incorrect. To counter this, slightly drop the hips and start to step forwards, this movement brings the drawing hand in line with the grip, next bring out the weapon in one fluid movement as you complete the step.

DRAW A WEAPON WITH FLUID MOTION

Ejection port check

After each time the weapon is fired, turn it on its side and inspect the exhaust port to make sure that it is not jammed or fouled. Then turn the weapon back to its original position, performing muzzle discipline, and reholster it.

The double tap

The term "double tap" needs little introduction as it is featured in many films. The general idea is to shoot twice at the enemy, the first shot being rapid, and then to aim and fire again. This technique is often identified by the saying "two in the body one in the head" (making three shots in two bursts); however the main idea is to place two bursts into the body to put an enemy down.

Controlled pair

The controlled pair is similar to the double tap, however it is done at a slightly slower speed and with more accuracy. Of course the aim is to train in the double tap until there is almost no delay between shots. The highest level of proficiency is a double tap with extreme accuracy and speed.

Shooting multiple targets

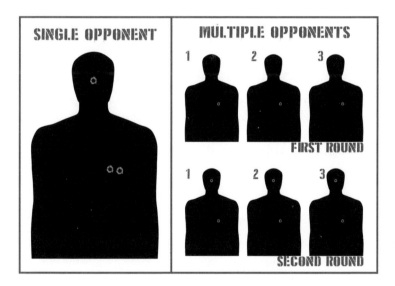

Some security teams prefer a different method to the double tap when dealing with multiple targets. The alternative version is to shoot each person once in the body as this allows a gunman to acquire the upper hand as "double tapping" multiple

SINGLE OPPONENT - STANDARD DOUBLE TAP
MULTIPLE OPPONENTS - ONE ROUND IN EACH TARGET,
THEN RETURN FOR SECOND ROUND

enemy targets takes up too much time. This method of a single shot to each enemy first allows for a gunman to disable or at least reduce the firing accuracy of the enemy which gives them time to return to the each assailant and to then place a second shot to terminate them.

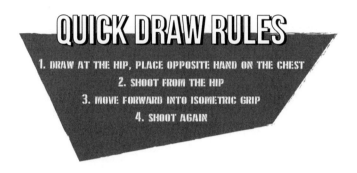

The truth about the quick draw

Quick drawing skills in Japanese swordsmanship are known as *iai*, *iaijutsu* and *batto*. The now popular art of *iaido* is a spiritual representation of sword drawing connected to Zen. Originally *iaido* sword draws would have been fast and deadly. It is not possible that it would have been performed in the slow manner that they are today. In comparison, today, a gun being used in hostile areas would never be drawn slowly—you would be killed in a very short time. Over time, *iai* fast response skills evolved into a slower art form based on Zen. In old Japan, *iai* or *iaijutsu* was a fast art which was honed to give a person excellent defensive skills in life threatening situations. The following examples show the various types of both modern gun and old sword draws.

Quick draw skills with a pistol

There are some outstanding fast draw pistol experts today who are a perfect example of just how fast a human can be with a weapon. And while the samurai would have been slower due to the length of the blade, they would still be very quick. For a pistol, it is best to draw fast and shoot from the hip to gain time, then move the weapon up to an isometric pressure grip and shoot a second time with more accuracy. In the following images, where appropriate, a boxed line has been placed around figures on the left of the image to show the situation a gunman would be in and where the aggressor would be standing. The movement is then shown by a series of single figures to the right.

The t-shirt draw—Practice lifting the shirt and drawing in a fluid motion.

The jacket hook and draw—Use a hand as a hook to pull back the jacket and then draw on the enemy.

Drawing to the holster side—When the enemy is to your side, draw, shoot, step backwards and fire again.

Draw to the opposite side—When the enemy is on the opposite side of your drawing hand, draw the weapon and aim across the body, making sure that the empty hand is on the chest or opposite shoulder so that it is out of the way of the weapon.

Draw to the rear—When an enemy is behind, draw and shoot directly backwards, but then step away from the enemy and fire again.

Draw–shoot–reload—When your magazine runs dry, release and drop the magazine, move from your position and keep on the move. At the same time reload, and without looking, fire again once ready. This is an extremely quick technique wish only allows for a very small time loss. It should be performed on the move while looking at the enemy.

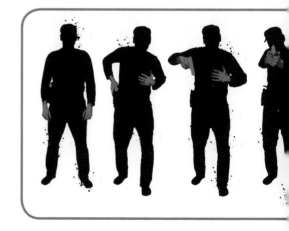

The up close hip draw—When the enemy is up close, use this draw to shoot from the hip, then follow up with more shots from a proper stance.

The face flick and draw—When the enemy is very close, strike upwards with the fingers or fist and use the distraction to shoot the enemy from the hip.

Quick draw skills with a sword

There are various schools in Japan with branches across the world who practice *iaido;* however, the numbers are very few. In fact, it is quite rare to find someone who practices *iaijutsu,* the fast-draw originator of *iaido.* As stated previously, the difference is that *iaido* is an art that has developed and focuses on both Zen and competition. It is more like a majestic demonstration of sword drawing with some strong bursts, whereas *iaijutsu* is the practical skill of drawing a sword in realistic defense.

These terms were only established in modern times. In the 20th century *iaido* (like all Japanese martial arts) was incorporated into a national organization with guidelines and prescribed regulations. Speed and practicality were replaced by grace, the second biggest change being that of seating. Many old schools—called *ko-ryu*—now practice their set forms from a seated position, but in most cases this seated fighting position was a later addition—the original sword draws created by the founder were performed while standing or walking. This means that many of the skills you observe in these old schools have drastically changed from their original intention but their essence does remain hidden.

IAIDŌ   IAIJUTSU

PRIMARY EVIDENCE

For close combat or sword fighting, there is no way to describe how to do such things at length here. Therefore, just be sure to always train yourself with: kenjutsu–swordsmanship, iai–sword drawing and so on. Tactics always depend on the time and place.

—*The Book of Ninja* (1676)

The following sword quick draw skills are taken from Tamiya-Ryu (Wakayama branch) with the permission of the head of that branch (Ikeda-Sensei) while others are from the Natori-Ryu school. Again, the situation has been presented in a boxed outline on the left and the steps on the right.

To cut the wrists from an overhead attack—The enemy comes at you with their sword from above, the response is to draw and cut across their wrists in a quick, fluid motion.

Drawing to attack the left—When a person at the side draws their weapon, move backwards and draw, avoid their cut and then move in to eliminate them.

Draw to the rear—When a person grabs your drawing hand and restrains it, force out your stomach to hold the sword in its belt and then use the opposite hand to draw.

The punch and draw—When an enemy takes hold of your weapon handles, strike them hard and repeatedly in the face until they let go, then draw and strike with the blade.

Locking the enemy arm with your hilt—When an enemy to the left is about to draw their sword on you, use the hilt of your own sword in a pushing manner to lock down their arm, then draw and cut them, followed by a stab.

Weapon Use: Knife

The first thing you need to understand about knife fighting is that if you have to fight with a knife, things have gone very wrong. The only thing that could be worse is having to resort to unarmed combat. Knife fighting is extremely dangerous, bloody and violent—there should be zero reliance on sophisticated or "flashy"

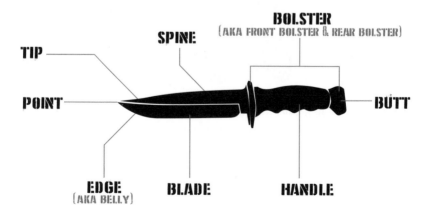

BOLSTER
(AKA FRONT BOLSTER & REAR BOLSTER)

SPINE

TIP

POINT

BUTT

EDGE
(AKA BELLY)

BLADE

HANDLE

moves. In essence, stop a stab or attack, control the weapon (never losing that control) and then terminate the enemy.

1. Stop.
2. Control.
3. Kill.

As the medieval warrior Hans Talhoffer said: "Now we take up the dagger, God preserve us all."

Stabbing and slicing

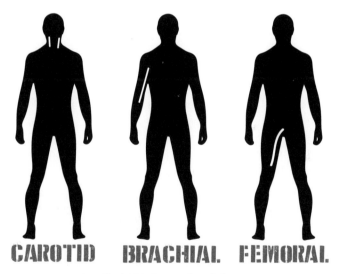

CAROTID　　BRACHIAL　　FEMORAL

The body's three major arteries.

Stabbing and slicing is easy—just hold the knife and stab or slice. Everyone, from a battered wife to the unskilled criminal can manage this without any training. However, people often defend their vital points very well so a stab that has immediate effect can sometimes be difficult unless performing a sudden onslaught of blows. While effective, this will leave you open to be easily stabbed in return before the enemy goes down. A controlled approach with feints is better than risking your own death. Try aiming for the eyes, throat, groin and lungs. The heart is a difficult target because of the protection around it. A stab to the heart is normally given by samurai as a *coup de grace* to a warrior that is already defeated.

Never let go

During knife fighting, if you manage to grip the wrist of the enemy do not let it go. Use that focal point to move around and apply your techniques from that position. Letting go of the enemy's knife hand is very dangerous—once you have control keep control, lock or restrict the enemy and then perform a final blow. Never let go unless the situation means your immediate death.

NEVER LET GO

Let them bleed out

A stab to the stomach feels like a punch and will not put a person down quick enough. Of course the opponent will be in dire need of medical aid but that will be after they have had time to kill you; therefore, if possible, slice through an artery to bleed them out. The major arteries that should be attacked are shown previously. Remember to restrain them before or after a cut and then keep them restrained until they expire.

Three stabs are better than one

When stabbing, focus on hitting an area that will slow or stop the enemy as quickly as possible, but also perform three stabs to the same position or area. Of course it would be too difficult to stab the exact same place three times; however, the point is to open up wounds in one area so that the damage is massive at that point. A person can be stabbed multiple times in multiple locations and take time to die or

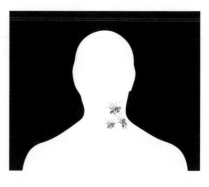

they may even recover, but stabbing in the same area multiple times will encourage massive blood loss and cause them immediate problems. On the third strike, twist and rip out the knife to cause more damage. It is important to remember that you can make multiple attacks of three, do not just stab three times and finish. It is essential to stab three times in one area, then move to a new area and stab again three times until the enemy is down. Stabbing three times is an old samurai teaching.

Attack the carotid then slice the femoral

When engaged in ground combat, and you are in a position to move your right arm, while holding the enemy with your left in a choke—either facing up or down—draw your dagger and attempt to attack the throat. This will make the enemy move to defend their neck area. As the enemy moves to defend their neck, quickly move the blade down to inside of their thigh and slice the femoral artery. People often focus on defending their throat but forget that the femoral artery is only one slice away and death is near. After doing this, maintain the chokehold and allow them to bleed out.

Support the blade with the hand

When up close with a blade of any length, be it sword, machete or dagger, if extra strength is needed to deepen or strengthen a cut, move in and support the back of the blade with your hand, then use the body in a fluid motion to add pressure to the cut. For example, when up close in a clinch, move the blade onto the body, preferably the carotid or brachial artery, and push the blade hard down, then use your body to perform the cut.

Escaping a bind

Two people fighting with knifes will often end up grabbing the wrist of the hand which holds the knife of the opponent and leaves a situation where both people hold each other's wrists. This can often end in a stalemate where both parties are trying to use strength to push the knife towards the other one in a form of wrestling match. In this situation, lift the knee closest to your knife hand, lift it up to *their* wrist and then force your knee outwards, pushing against the inside of *their* wrist. This will break the hold the enemy has on your knife hand while you maintain a strong hold on the enemy knife hand. Use this quick break to then stab them three times.

LIFT STAB JACKET

The first goal here would be to deal with the enemy's knife.
This image illustrates the final part of combat only.

Lift the stab jacket

If the enemy has a stab jacket on, engage quickly and use your free hand to reach down and grab the bottom of the stab jacket, lift it up with extreme force and then stab below into the gut.

The collar bone hook

Reverse the grip on the knife and during a scuffle, insert the blade into the enemy behind the collar bone, and use this to pull the enemy down, remove the blade and then stab the enemy three times in the closest vital area.

BEHIND COLLAR BONE

Hand-to-hand Combat

Hand-to-hand combat is combat between individuals or groups where no projectile weapons are fired; therefore it mainly consists of bladed and bludgeoning weapons. Up until the 20th century traditional martial arts such as the various *kung-fu* schools, *jujutsu*, *karate*, *aikido*—which are unarmed today—actually had some focus on weapon fighting. It was later when they dropped the focus on weapons and moved towards sports or demonstration.

Japanese hand-to-hand combat

When considering Japanese hand-to-hand combat many people often think of *aikido*, *karate*, *jujutsu* etc.; however, *aikido* is a 20th century art, *karate* is Okinawan and only came to mainland Japan as a popular art in the 20th century, and while *jujutsu* as a term does trace its roots to samurai times it was used much later in samurai history as a label. In addition to this, Brazilian Jujutsu (BJJ) is still very much a Japanese art, as the Gracie family developed it in a time when the art was still practical. Its effectiveness is because it was not warped by Japan's 20th century move towards demonstration and tradition over application after World War II.

Earlier samurai times tended to use the following words for hand-to-hand and unarmed combat:

- *Sojutsu* (槍術)—spearsmanship
- *Kenjutsu* (剣術)—swordsmanship
- *Iai* (居合)—fast response sword drawing
- *Shuriken-jutsu* (手裏剣術)—hidden blades and throwing weapons
- *Kusarigama-jutsu* (鎖鎌術)—skills with sickle and chain
- *Kusaridama-jutsu* (鎖玉術)—skills with ball and chain
- *Kumiuchi* (組討)—grappling and striking
- *Jujutsu* (柔術)—close combat
- *Taijutsu* (体術)—close combat
- *Torimono-jutsu* (捕物術)—capturing skills

Shinobi did not develop a specific form of their own hand-to-hand combat that was peculiar to them; they practiced the forms above within their own families or schools and each area, person or tradition had their own similarities and differences. Make sure to understand that each shinobi practiced mainstream samurai combat, not a separate form that was only used by shinobi and always remember *ninjutsu* is the art of spying and infiltration, not unarmed combat.

Basic hand-to-hand combat skills

It is not a fair fight—Hand-to-hand combat should never be a fair fight outside of the ring. The point of training and of tactics is to push the odds in your favor before the fight starts. When fighting for your life, you do not want a 50/50 chance of death; you have to use everything in your power from weapons, groups, situations, position and surprise to ensure those odds of success are very high and not equal. Anyone can kill anyone; training changes the chance of success in your favor.

Gain control—Hand-to-hand combat is about gaining control of a person, restricting them and then taking them out. Often hand-to-hand combat may erupt when weapons have failed or two people come on each other suddenly in small area. In such a case, the key here is to take control of the opponent, both in balance and movement and then to draw your sidearm and fire into them.

Attack from cover—If there is a chance to take the enemy by surprise and stab them from behind or from cover or inside a group, take it. When a pistol cannot be used or there is a weapon jam, move in quick with a blade and stab each vital area three times. Knives can be fast on the draw and should be used when there is an issue with the sidearm.

This image is abstract and reality would not be so obvious. The key
focus is to be unseen and then attack without the target seeing you.

If alone, have a short sword which is double edged and with no hand-guard, this is to be used as a dagger that is kept inside of the kimono. Next wait at an appropriate place for someone to come by, grab the person by the chest and hold the dagger in the right hand in a reverse grip and quickly cut their throat.

—The Lost Samurai School (17th century)

Unarmed Combat

Unarmed combat is when things have moved past the stage of *hand-to-hand combat* with weapons—either all weapons have been dropped or there were no weapons involved to begin. The modern world places a massive amount of emphasis on unarmed combat but in truth, the ancient ninja, like paramilitary groups, had no real situation where this was a required skill. Almost all situations, both in medieval Japan and today, when working behind enemy lines or in battle, weapons will always be used. If it has reached a situation where it has come down to unarmed combat then something has gone extremely wrong in the planning or execution of the task. Undercover agents may have no weapons on them; however, most likely if captured there would be no use for unarmed combat as they will be deep inside enemy lines and have little chance of escape.

This does not mean that there is no need to train in unarmed combat. It is actually a fundamental requirement for good movement—it promotes a proper use of the body, gives a person stability in their activities and may help in a few cases, but overall it is a part of basic training that should be maintained at a certain level. However, it should be understood that a focus on unarmed fighting is not needed for a modern paramilitary agent—concentration should be on armed combat.

KICKING　　　KNEEING　　　PUNCHING　　　THROWING

Unarmed combat should be direct, quick, disabling and violent but not based on strength alone. The illustration above shows the basic methods of unarmed combat, but it is assumed that you would have basic training in this area before moving on to specialized training.

Arresting Skills

Arresting skills were known in old Japan as *torimono*. If a person had committed a crime and fled, or if a lord ordered the death of one of his retainers, he would call upon the services of the shinobi, experts in tracking and hunting people or someone who possessed specialized arresting skills. This can of course be done as a single person, but the samurai had no qualms about ganging up on one man (the idea of the samurai fair fight is rooted in our misunderstanding of samurai honor); therefore, often a team may have been sent out to capture or kill the enemy, of which there are various ways to do this. The following sections will give a brief overview of the basic areas; however, be aware that this subject can be considered in great depth and did become an art form in itself. Many schools developed around this area.

The use of gas

As poison powders and choking agents are thrown into a room, the occupants leave the room blinded and choking. Just as how gas is used today, in old Japan the agent stood away from the door and made arrests as they left the room or executed the targets .

The use of fire

Very few people will remain in a building and allow themselves to burn to death; therefore, if you need someone out of a building then burn it down. Prepare your team at the exits and be ready to capture or neutralize them.

BURN IT DOWN

Take the bloody doors off

If you have the ability to, remove the doors of a building. In old Japan this would be done with cattle or horses while today vehicles such as jeeps or tractors are used. Use them to pull off the doors and move in. In this situation the enemy will remain inside and may kill any hostages they may have. This skill is used for direct assaults.

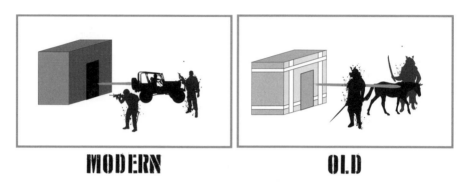

Multiple angle and multiple level infiltration

If your team is large enough, prepare ladders and climbing gear and have various groups come in through different doors and at different levels of a building. Make a coordinated attack from all angles and move the enemy into the center or capture or take them out on the way in.

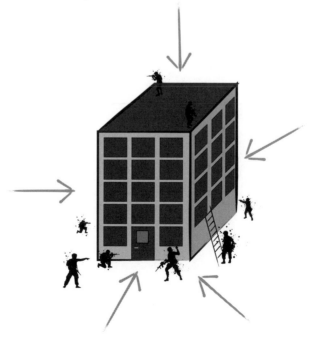

Secret communication

Find a way to secretly communicate with one of the people inside a building and attempt to bribe them in exchange for them betraying their comrades. Old shinobi scrolls say that this is difficult to do if there are close bonds between the people on the inside, such as family ties or military experience.

Boiling water

If the enemy is in the open and are cornered but they are too strong to bring down, start fires and prepare boiling water. Move in as a team, throw boiling water over them and they will buckle. Also, you can use stones or heavy sticks that, when thrown in unison, will cause the enemy to defend themselves so the team can run in and make the grab.

The tools of capture

In old Japan there were different types of capture tools used to ensnare, corner and entangle the enemy. The modern forms of these tools are still used today in parts of Japan and similar tools are used elsewhere. The older versions were much more vicious and had spiked collars or sharp edges used to tear the flesh.

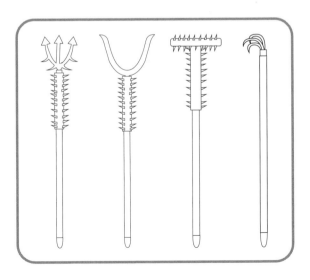

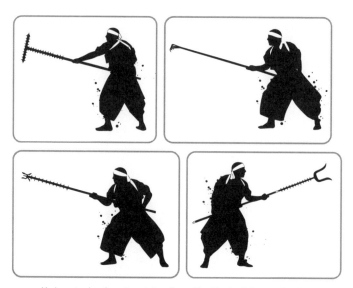

Various tools of capture taken from *The Book of Samurai* series.

The hook and rope

The use of the hook and rope in old Japan was a special skill and samurai trained in the ways of restraint. The use of hook and rope can be broken down into two stages: first, capture with a thin rope and sharp hook and second, when the enemy is subdued, secure them with a thicker binding rope.

Stage one: capture with cord and hook—The basic rules for hooking with the smaller cord is to move in with speed and pierce the hook into an area where the enemy can be controlled. Next, pull them off balance and tangle them up in the rope. Neatness is not used at this stage; the main aim is to ensnare them and restrain them, ready for correct binding.

These three areas are the targets used by the Natori-Ryu school.

Criminals can also be captured with the use of a staff and rope loop, it was used in old Japan to loop over the arm or head of a criminal, then twisted, tightened and used to restrain.

Stage two: the complex art of binding—The art of correctly binding a restrained person is a complex one. Many books, scrolls and lessons are dedicated to this art alone. The main point to remember is that the enemy is already pinned and this part of the binding process can be performed much slower and with deliberate movements. The opponent can then be lead away on a lead and gagged when needed. Remember that at first the opponent is restricted with a hook and thin cord. Only when you have control of them a larger rope and complex knots is to be used.

Gags

After an enemy has been bound, sometimes they need to be gagged. The image here are examples of the gags found in Natori-Ryu in their encyclopedia on samurai arms and equipment. An enemy could be gagged to stop them from giving a position away, or to stop them from shouting when being led back to the lord's compound.

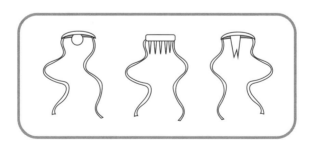

Invasion and defense

Invasion and defense are the central tasks for shinobi on a military campaign but are less so for those shinobi who are working undercover as spies in enemy territory. On a military campaign, a shinobi would be on the move with an army, setting up camp each time they moved on, creating bamboo fences and ditches. They would defend the area at night and infiltrate the enemy camp in no man's land. Also, because the arts of the ninja are used in civilian life for revenge and robbery, much of *shinobi no jutsu* is based on infiltration and burglary. Imagining military compounds today is not so difficult but what you should take care to do is not imagine the samurai house as a "home." Often it was more of a compound and complex of buildings. One big difference in old Japan was that in the years prior to 1600, the samurai increasingly lived in the countryside with their own fortified manor houses which had a collection of farms under their control. These fortified manor houses were very much military compounds and were the centers of warrior families. Infiltrating them was akin to entering the compound of a warlord in modern South America or a tribal complex in Africa today. From the year 1600 onwards, samurai tended to stay more and more with the lord in castle towns, living in walled enclosures in certain wards of the city. Therefore, do not fall into the trap of thinking that a "samurai house" was a home as we know it today.

Defending a Compound

Later, the shinobi became more like castle guards and night watchmen. Many of them would have maintained their family tradition as shinobi; however, historical records show that in these later times, *Iga-mono* (men of Iga) and *Koka-mono* (men of Koka) simply patrolled the watch grounds of castles and areas close to the lord. There is no doubt that covert activity did occur and that the ninja were used in periods of peace; however, more and more of their duties lay in patrol and as watchmen. This stems from their expertise in defending military compounds from other shinobi since ninja knew how to effectively infiltrate. Documentation from the early 1600s shows that military camps used *shinobi-shu* (ninja groups) to guard the lord.

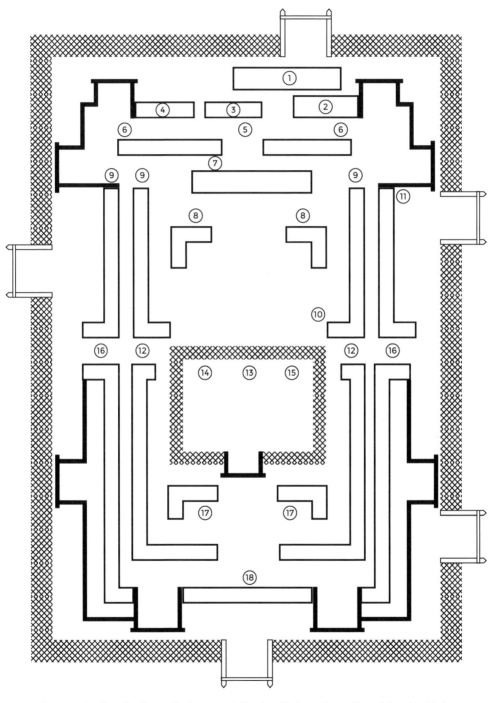

A camp setup from the Gunpo Jiyoshu manual. Number 17 shows the position of the *shinobi-shu*.

Spiked defenses

Spiked defenses are a simple but often needed option for home defense. They do not deter infiltrators but they could create hazards to be overcome. In old Japan they were often used but the shinobi had ways to get around them. Spiked defenses come in two main forms.

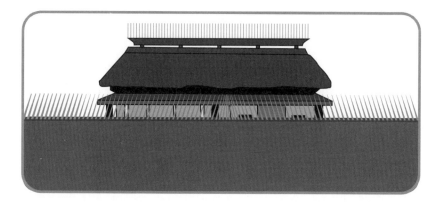

1. Spikes on buildings—Today we have barbed wire, spiked fences, electrified fences and broken glass that is strewn atop walls. In old Japan they had spikes called *shinobi-gaeshi* (忍返). They were either placed vertically along walls or rooftops or horizontally, anchored to walls to stop people climbing up. They were made of both bamboo and metal. Shinobi scrolls mention multiple ways to defeat these spikes:

1. Saw or snap the spikes off.
2. Place cut-down bamboo over the spikes.
3. Throw a heavy cloth over the spikes.

Modern forces still use the third method by throwing a ballistics blanket over a fence and climbing over it.

PRIMARY EVIDENCE

忍返心得之事

Shinobi-gaeshi Kokoroe no Koto

Things to be aware about concerning defensive spikes

To cross over walls which have shinobi-gaeshi—*defensive spikes upon them, know that the spikes may be broken off with a nail remover or alternatively, bamboo cylinders can be placed over the spikes. Furthermore, there is a tradition called* nunoshiki—*spreading cloth.*

—*The Book of Samurai series* (17th century)

2. Spiked Caltrops—Caltrops are universally used, from the medieval world all the way to modern times, where spiked extendable platforms are placed in roads to stop oncoming vehicles. Extreme-

ly large versions of these are even used to stop beach landings.

The shinobi used caltrops in three ways:

1. Placed in certain positions along an escape route.
2. Scattered in an area to close it off.
3. Attached to strings and either placed in an area or trailed behind them as they run.

Both attackers and defenders used caltrops in many situations. A shinobi infiltrator would position them at doorways or in halls in the enemy house so that if anyone woke up and gave chase they would tread upon them. They also used vast quantities of them to block off roads in night raids or laid them as traps for ambushes. They could also scatter them behind in an emergency, or trail them behind on a string. Likewise, defenders would place them at the foot of walls to injure people jumping down or, if they knew it was a night of attack, they would position them around the area themselves.

There were three main ways to bypass shinobi caltrops:

1. Use a shuffling walk (*suriashi*) to push them out of the way.
2. Use a brush to sweep them away quickly.
3. Hold a spear on the floor and move it from side to side, sweeping them out of the way.

Alarm systems

Alarm systems advance as technology develops. In old Japan alarm systems were based on "listening scouts" or "listening patrols," called *togiki* by Fujibayashi-sensei. *Togiki* were set up in certain positions, normally outside the camp, and were "armed" with wooden warning clappers. At further distances they used signal fires and rockets.

Dogs

Dogs are the bane of an infiltrator and can smell a human "a mile away." The use of guard dogs was essential for detecting the enemy in the past. Stray dogs could also have been useful to have outside camps creating two waves of animals—those outside the fence scavenging for food and those inside guarding the area. One common method that was used to train guard dogs was to feed the dog with a colored rag attached to the wrist. If the dog took the food when this rag was *not* tied around the feeder's wrist the dog was beaten. This was done

until the dog learned that it should only take food from a hand with a specific colored rag. This way when an enemy infiltrated and attempted to give the dog food laced with poison, the dog would never take the food.

Patrols

Patrols should be carried out both inside and outside of the compound and can be performed at irregular times. These patrols should be divided into light and dark patrols. A light patrol is a patrol that walks around the camp in the open with a light source. They search all the nooks and crannies for the enemy and are a deterrent. They should be well armed and ready to capture anyone they find that is suspicious. Dark patrols are defenders that use no lights, do not operate in the open and who wait until after the light patrol has passed to move. Normally an intruder will wait for the light patrol to pass and then they will infiltrate in the gaps between patrols. Dark patrols are there to fill that gap and not be seen, apprehending anyone trying to infiltrate between the light patrols. The camp commander should create fresh passwords for the light and dark patrols every day so that if they meet at night then they can identify themselves as friendly and not be mistaken for enemy shinobi. These passwords must change every day.

PRIMARY EVIDENCE

One samurai from another troop was wandering around like me but found his troop in the end and so he tried to join them. However, he only had one identifying mark on his shoulder but it had been torn off save for only a little of the cloth. Also, he didn't have the other two kinds of identifying marks and when asked to say the password, as he was fluttered, and could not remember the code word, each troop he came to shunned him and moved him on. In time they began saying the enemy had mixed in with us, in the end he was beheaded.

—Samurai War Stories (17th century)

Passwords and security

Passwords and security are essential in areas with limited technology as they were in medieval Japan. Where only the face and uniform will allow recognition, other forms of passwords and identification markers are required. The following sections highlight those types:

The paper stamp—In this method, small stamps are created and sections of paper are cut. If a squad of 50 men is going out on patrol, then 51 pieces of stamped paper must be made. Each member of the patrol takes one on the way out and then hands it back on their return. This means that anyone trying to get in will become stuck at the gate when they cannot provide the paper. The stamps picture soemthing simple, such as a Chinese character or an image of a moon, stars or animal. However, they only should be used that night, so no infiltrator can forge the wooden stamp in that short time. The paper is destroyed or stored and a new set given out to each large patrol the next night.

Dual passwords—Multiple stages of passwords are required; these are normally done in a "challenge-answer" format. For example, when a guard says "moon" the response could be "stars," or they can be less direct—the correct response to the challenge "King Arthur" could be "Merlin," as the answer to "moon" is normally only a few, but the answer to King Arthur can be many. These passwords are created by the administrators and distributed daily. However, that is only the main army password. Each troop could then create their own password so that men from their own army cannot become mixed up with their inner group. This can be broken down even further and each five man squad can have their own. In addition to this, special one-use passwords and paper stamps are given out to night raid parties or individual shinobi. This means that a warrior may have to remember up to four or more different password combinations per day, each set changing every 24 hours.

Passwords with signals—There are also passwords that include movements, for example sitting down when speaking or pulling at the left ear. This is normally performed inside the square killing zone of a castle gate (see page 86).

Passwords on the move—Another password set is to have a command word inside of a troop of men and upon that command word, everyone kneels down, this is done to identify if anyone has infiltrated the group at night and on the move. Those who have infiltrated the squad will not know the password and will be left standing when the rest of the men have squatted down. It is then easy to identify infiltrators in the troop and execute them. Remember this could be hundreds of men on the move throughout the night.

Armor identification markers—For samurai who are raiding or acting as a shinobi group at night, the ring on the back of their helmet is then used to attach a marker with their name or a troop marker. These can also be put on the shoulders and other parts of the armor. The troop will check each other in a "buddy system" before they move out and have a few identification markers upon them. These help them quickly identify friend from foe. Again, these change. Shinobi will quickly steal these from the dead to use for infiltration that night, or like a predator they will target any troop member who strays from the group to gain a marker and take that man's place.

Light

With modern floodlights it is easy to light a compound and defend it. However, you have to keep in mind that there is a cost to keeping areas lit, from burning wood in old Japan to power from generators or electrical lines today. Electrical lines are a bad option because there i a reliance on power is brought from outside and any "lifeline" that leads outside of your camp is a weakness. Shadows are the infiltrator's dream and ancient samurai ways teach that it is best to have no shadows in which an enemy can lurk. The following points concern lights when defending a compound:

No shadows—Create buildings and walls with an idea in mind to not cast too many shadows nor to have parts where the enemy can hide. Flush, curved and longer straight walls are better that hard angles. The outside of the wall should be designed to give the best arcs of fire, meaning that there will be corners and nooks and crannies, but the inside of the wall should be as open as possible to not allow shadows to form and to help with swift movement of troops along the inside.

Camp lights—In old Japan, outside of light pollution and when the moon is new (meaning black), it was dark, very dark indeed, and a hand-held torch can be problematic. A modern flashlight is powerful but only shines in one direction. An old torch projects light on all sides but is not as bright. In old Japan, be it in a static compound or in a movable camp, the army would use special recipes to create a high intensity burning solid fuel and then place it in iron basket frames. These frames would then be erected and would light over an area, similar to the idea of a modern floodlight. These would be positioned just inside each other's radius of light so that a blanket of illumination covered the area or in positions to expel shadows.

A battle camp torch, an iron basket on a bracket to illuminate over shadowed areas.

"Monkey" light—A "monkey" light is a burning torch attached to a rope (in a manner so that it does not burn the rope). This is lowered down the outsides of the external compound walls, up and down in dark areas. This is done so that the "light patrol" can pour light into all the dark shadowy areas outside of the camp.

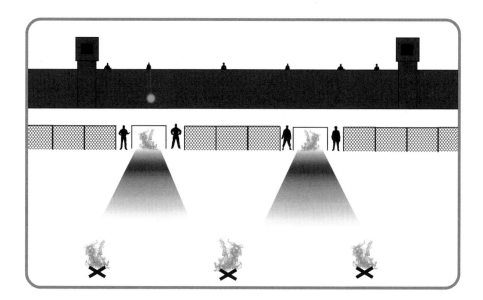

External fires—The external wall should not be a divide between you and the enemy. Most people consider this to be the case. Instead have an ironclad command of the external areas of your camp. No one should be allowed to just walk up to the walls. The only time this is possible is when a larger force has committed to a siege and forced you inside of your own perimeter. The external area should be full of guards, patrols, and fires. An external fire comes in two types—the first is closer to the wall and is large with armed guards, the second type is further out and unattended, except for personnel who visit them at intervals to refuel, or they are just left to burn as long as they can.

The second and most external line is easy enough to understand. It is just a ring of fires outside your camp; however, the external fires which are closer to the wall are used to form a second perimeter around the camp. Originally these were made with clay and had walls that reached up seven feet. Today these can be custom built for the purpose. They are cuboids that have an open front and air vents

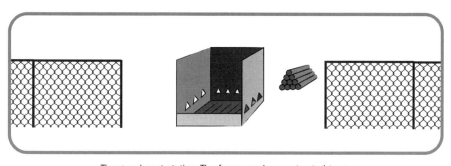

The guard post station. The fence can be constructed to go around the back of the fire with a gate for entry.

at the lower sections. To either side is a fence or ditch—the ditch will often have sand added at the bottom which is smooth, this is done to show the footprints of intruders—and armed guards are either behind the fence or off to the sides so that they stay in the dark. They will feed the fire all night until morning with a change of guards on a rota. This requires a lot of power or wood for fires and means that an isolated camp has only a certain timeframe it can operate like this and move on, or it is permanent with an infrastructure that builds up stores for times of need.

Trip wires and noise creation devices

Trip wires and noise creation devices are not to be relied upon; however they constitute that extra level of defense, the same as spikes. They do not stop infiltrators but they help to make it difficult for them.

Trip wires—Trip wires are not simply wires. They should be used along with a complex system of pathways known only to your troops. The following are the options for trip wires:

- In an area you do not expect a direct attack, but need to defend, have a network of crossing tripwires placed between stakes helping form a barrier against the enemy. In addition, use barriers of thorny branches staked to the ground.
- Use a network of tripwires on the bed of a river to trip troops crossing and to cause them to have to wait and dismantle the barrier before they can pass.
- Use a combination of tripwires and pot holes or trenches, so that the enemy cannot just step over them. This gives you a system of: wire and then ditch, and again wire and then ditch, making it difficult for troops to move at speed across this wire and ditch complex.
- Create hidden trip wires in areas that are deemed easy for infiltrators to move in. Attach bells to them so that they ring an alarm when tripped.
- Use single trip wires around a house to trip up single intruders. These should also have bells attached to them.

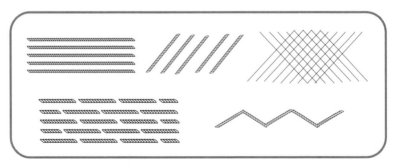

Various trip wire formations taken from *The Book of Samurai* series.

Noise creation devices—These are simple set ups where an intruder triggers something to create noise. In old Japan this was often a rope tied to a bucket of stones which would fall on to a hard surface, or a system of wires and bells or even cockle shells in the garden to alert if anyone has entered the area. Use anything that will clang, rattle or bang when triggered. Today, this can be things such as flares attached to trip wires etc.

The leg smashing trap—Another noise creation system is the leg smashing trap. This is a strong piece of flexible material, drawn back which is released when triggered by tripping on a wire. This will hit the legs of the infiltrator and cause them to cry out in pain.

PRIMARY EVIDENCE

Harahata-barai shank sweepers should be prepared on the inside or the outside of your own mansion and on every route you expect the enemy shinobi will come from.

—The Book of Ninja (1676)

Traps

Traps are used by shinobi and against shinobi. Often a position will have a trap system to warn of any infiltrators in the area, or to injure, trap or create nose. The following traps are a basic outline of the situations used.

Far from the camp—Away from the camp, the areas surrounding should be scouted for the most likely routes that an infiltrator will take. In this area, pitfall traps, leg traps etc., should be placed on the path. Only those scouting the area should know they exist as there is no need for regular troops to be there. If it is an open plain where the enemy would advance in force, multiple and large pitfalls should be dug and covered over. These should be made with enemy transport in mind, from a horse, to a bike to a tank. Defend open plains or hills with everything from trenches all the way down to small traps and tunnels.

Around the camp—Traps should be set in the area immediately around the camp; however, these should be known to everyone and can have a secret mark on them which is obvious to those who know but not to those who are infiltrating in low light or at speed.

Inside the camp—There can be pitfall traps placed on the upper walkways of a camp if possible, but these are large engineering tasks and should be well known or marked out for internal troops. These were sometimes used in old Japan. At the siege of Shimabara it is said that Koka shinobi fell into such traps.

Gates

Gates to a camp are the weak points in the fortress, so there are set rules to follow when creating them. The following principles are found in most fortresses worldwide.

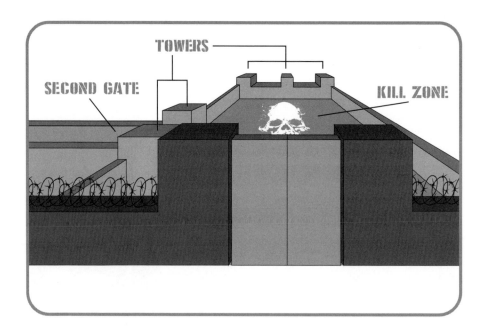

Towers to the sides—There must be a structure on either side of the gate that allows an armed guard to shoot down at people approaching and must offer protection to the guard. These can be anything from scaffolding with cover all the way to the full medieval castle.

Strong gates—The gates themselves must be reinforced and very strong. They must be lockable from the inside and they should have the ability to be barred quickly and reinforced with struts. Shooting ports can be put in them for small arms fire, but there must be a cap on the inside that can be shut.

Small holes and secret shooting points should be either hidden well or have the ability to be closed.

Never have a direct approach—The road leading up to the gate should never be a direct approach, it should always be offset and have ditches, banks or obstructions on either side. This stops being from using heavy vehicles and rams from gaining momentum. Likewise, the inside of the compound should not carry on in a straight line but should turn to one side.

Blockage walls—On the outside of a gate should be a reinforced wall, this can be angled or curved, it has a duel purpose, first is to spread the approaching enemies to either side when they attack and second is to give your own troops shielding when they exit.

Killing zones—On the inside of the gate should be an enclosed area, this has vantage points and shooting ports. If the enemy penetrates the gate they need to be trapped between the arch of fire from the gate turrets and the turrets in the killing zone and also from the shooting points.

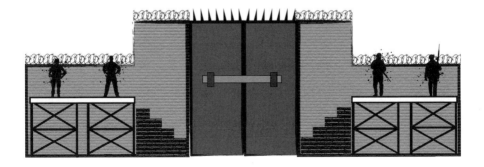

Second gate—On the inner side of the killing zone should be another lesser gate that is closed when under attack and keeps the enemy inside a kill zone if they break through. This will have platforms behind the wall.

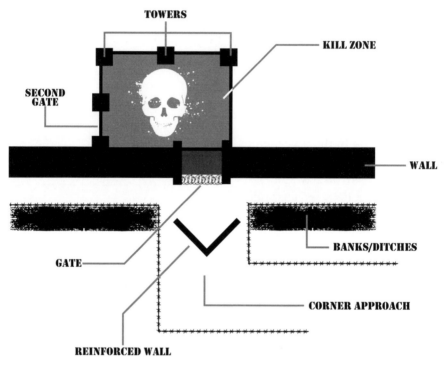

An overview of the principles of gate security.

Altogether, the above constitutes a single gateway. There will be multiples of these gateways around the compound, unless it is small and only has a single main gate. In that case have a smaller defended rear but guard it well.

The area outside—Immediately outside the compound, the area should be open and visible with no buildings nor any trees to allow the enemy to hide. If there are buildings or a local population, then on a serious enemy approach, destroy the town and cut down any trees and use them for the compound internals or for fuel. Either send the population away or bring them inside. If local populations are established outside the camp, only allow them to build out of materials that can be burned down with ease or which offer no protection to the enemy.

Multiple layers

Compounds should have multiple layers and be structured like castles. The basic principle is to follow multiple layers (known as *maru* in Japanese). These have a series of gates leading all the way to the main keep; however, these gates are always offset from each other and they never have a direct path between them. Turns and killing zones fill the way with vantage points for defenders. A compound or fortress should be on a height and it should be multi-layered.

Watch systems

Watch systems are guards that take up position for a certain amount of time and look out and defend the compound. The following are the general rules to be followed regarding guard houses and watch patrols.

Mix the experienced with the inexperienced—Experience individuals who have seen battle or performed their duties many times should be mixed in with those that are less inexperienced. Inexperienced individuals will drink, laugh, gamble and generally entertain themselves when performing a task in which 99.9% of the time there is downtime or there is no emergency. This is a "catch 22" situation. Infiltrators are looking for gaps in defenses, so the more vigilant the guard, the less likely there will be an infiltration; however, the less actual infiltration attempts the more the guards will become lax and infiltration attempts will occur. The key focus is to have experienced men maintain a vigilant guard so that there are no attempts by the enemy to infiltrate.

Length of watch—Each watch should short, maybe 2 hours long each, resulting in 4 watches in the hours of darkness. Of course watches are maintained 24 hours a day, but nighttime is the time most infiltrations will occur. Make sure to keep the watches short so that the guards do not become complacent.

Rotate the watches—Make sure that the system does not have the same people doing the same watch every day. Each person should move along the watch system until they have gone through all watches. Depending on the system used, there is normally one watch that is split in half so that it allows everyone to have a different watch schedule each day. This is called a "dog watch."

Move the watches—Guards should not look after the same part of the compound or fortress each watch. The reason for this is that guards may often be lower level, hired hands or conscripts. This means that spies can enter and become a part of the watch system, allowing them to communicate with the outside. Also, if the guards are kept in the same place, the enemy can bribe them with secret letters. Therefore, move the guards around but do not just move them one station along. Have those guards who are just about to change the watch report to the command station and assign them a new guard station each watch. Make sure they do not perform the same watch over and over or the next watch as well, which is too predictable. Keep the movement of the guards mixed.

Gambling, drinking and noise—Quiet should be maintained in the watch houses and guards should be vigilant. Guards only have to be on duty for a small amount of hours so strict discipline should be maintained in all watch towers, patrols and guard rooms.

Listening scouts—Position guards outside of the guardhouse in hidden areas nearby. These are called *togiki*—listening scouts or *those who hear from outside*. If a shinobi or infiltrator gets close to the guardhouse, the *togiki* listening scout nearby will hear them pass and when the infiltrator tries to cross the guard area. They can raise the alarm.

The drunken party ruse—When it is known for certain that an enemy will try to infiltrate the compound, create fake "parties" and lax guards. Take 60% of the watchmen and have they *pretend* to drink and gamble; take the other 40% and have them positioned nearby on listening and watching duty or also in the guardhouse but craftily looking out in secret. The infiltrator will try to pass by the party, using the noise to their advantage. On the given alarm, all guards return to a disciplined state and apprehend the infiltrator.

Maintain a constant signature

Signature means that which the enemy can see from the outside, such as watch fires, cooking fires, movement, sounds, and the like. A good shinobi is not just observing with their eyes but they are also listening to all things and looking at secondary elements. For example Fujibayashi-sensei tells us that a shinobi would observe the cooking fire regularly and then assess if there are any changes. For example, if there are *three* distinct periods of cooking fires that are observable day after day, but then on a different day there are *four* periods of fire, this means that the kitchens are preparing extra food, most likely for a night raid or for a foray out of the camp. This simple piece of information can let a shinobi know that troops will be leaving the compound soon, and preparations can be made. Therefore make sure to maintain a constant *signature* for the camp. If extra food is needed then cook it at the same time that the other meals are cooked, keep messengers, communications etc., the same and hide any extra movement inside that same signature profile.

Movement of the Principle

Depending on the situation, the infiltrator may be coming to perform an assassination on a specific person. They may also be there to create damage or steal. However, if it is an assassination, then the target is known as the "principle." Their whereabouts should be kept secret, even inside the camp. Not even the guards outside should know where the principle is kept. Sometimes it is the case that the "principle" is moved to a different room during the night. This may happen multiple times. The aim is to keep their position a secret and to not allow them to maintain the same routine each day. The outer wall guards the perimeter; the secondary fences create obstacles; and the inner compound layout should be secret to all but a few trusted retainers. Never take the same route; never eat at the same position; and do not allow your own troops nor the enemy troops to build up a movement profile.

Fake conversations

If you become aware that an enemy shinobi or infiltrator is close to the fences outside and that they are listening to troop conversation, do one of two things: either spread fake information to your own troops, allowing them to gossip about it, or have specific troop members perform fake conversations at the external wall. This will then be picked up by the enemy agent and reported back to their spy master. This is one way of using *converted spies*. Remember if you are attacking a compound, make sure that what you hear and what you see match up.

The fake raid routine

If two armies or forces are set up in temporary battle camps, close to each other and both aware of each other, they will have either shinobi working in the enemy camp or at least an agent observing the area outside. One option in this situation is to strike out from your base and hit the enemy in a night raid. They will of course have spies watching the area and have quick communication system back to HQ in place to warn of any approach. One strategy used in old Japan was to perform constant fake night raids to wear down the enemy. To perform this, split those troops that are *not* in the watch system into two halves. Take one half and have them prepare for a night raid. In old Japan this preparation involved the movement and tacking of horses, movement of flags or messengers, extra cooking fires etc.. Today this would be troops getting into vehicles, engines starting, floodlights outside being turned on, gates opening and other such actions. The spy watching the camp will report this movement and when that report gets back to camp, the enemy will wake their own troops up in anticipation for the attack. However, once the night raid is ready, cancel the operation and have your troops return to bed. Do this the next night but with the *other* half of the force. Never use the same troops two nights in a row as they will also get tired. Make sure that each raid party has a full night's sleep the next night and are not a part of any watch system. You can even have the troops move out and ride or drive near or around the enemy camp. This will keep the enemy up all night worrying, as they will not return to bed so quickly but will maintain a longer watch and become anxious. Doing this night after night will tire out the enemy until they become complacent or exhausted. At the correct time, make the intended night raid a real one and strike at them hard and with force. Lastly, never tell your own troops the plan, just make sure the administrative system allows 50% of the spare troops to have a full night's sleep at all time.

- Divide the force into three sections of unequal size.
- Night attack group 1 (50% of spare troops).
- Night attack group 2 (50% of spare troops).
- Group 3—the watch system.
- Divide the watch into a fair watch system.
- Day 1—have group 1 prepare for night attack.
- Day 2—have group 2 prepare for night attack.
- Run groups 1 and 2 in a rota system one night each.
- Wait for enemy to be exhausted.
- Attack when your own spies see fatigue in the enemy.

The previous selection of teachings are the basic areas for defending compounds. On the whole the group defending the compound should be quiet; there should be no way to tell what is happening inside the compound from the outside and the system in place should not be predictable. There should be multiple layers of security and there should be security that stretches way beyond the compound walls. A shinobi or infiltrator is looking for gaps. This is the meaning of the Japanese ideogram "*kan*" which is the root word for spying. It means to see light when a gate is open and therefore it is made up of the radicals of "gate" and "sun" showing that when a gate opens, a ray of light will come in through any gap. Therefore, keep security tight at all times and remember, a history of no infiltration is a good status to attain. Allowing guards to become lax because of zero infiltration only creates gaps for infiltrations to occur.

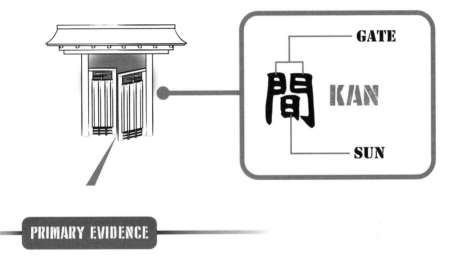

You may be certain of victory with the coming of dawn, but the moment you open the door. A ray of the moon will get in through it.
—*True Path of the Ninja* (1681)

Attacking a Compound

The above section dealt with defending a compound from the point of view of a shinobi infiltration, knowing how shinobi themselves would enter. The following sections will deal with how to infiltrate a compound based on the medieval ninja scrolls. The main focus for a shinobi is routine and observation. As mentioned above, the ideogram for "*kan*" means light coming through a gateway. There is no way to stop a light coming through a gap, therefore there is no way to stop a shinobi when they see a real opportunity. The task of the shinobi infiltrator is to observe gaps and act when those gaps appear, but at the same time to not fall victim to any traps put there by the enemy. The path of the shinobi is found in the concept of *kyojitsu*—which means detecting falsehood from truth.

The following list of teachings will reflect those given in the above section *Defending a Compound* but will be from the perspective of attacking. Because of this, they will be shorter and are to be considered points that build on the previous list. Any points of attack which are explained in the previous section are taken out here so as not to cause repetition, therefore both sections should be read as "two halves of the same coin."

Agreed takeover

An agreed takeover can be an arrangement instead of a siege. Often if you have a large enough force then you can inform the enemy of your intent as the size of your force will be overwhelming for them. Therefore, you may offer the enemy the possibility to surrender the base and to move out in safety. In old Japan this also happened with samurai castles as the outgoing samurai would bow to the incoming samurai after an agreement had been made. However, this moves into the realms of pure samurai warfare and conflicts on a larger scale. The following sections will focus on smaller attacks.

Observation, movement and routine

A shinobi or infiltrator will wait days or even weeks just observing a camp. This of course depends on the situation of the conflict; however, observation is key and alongside this is test infiltration, getting close and observing how the enemy troops move, what areas in their own position do they avoid, what alarm systems they have, what is there structure of emergency protocol etc. Observe the guard

dogs, check where spiked defenses are, etc. Remember, befriend and poison dogs or misdirect them by giving them something else to bark at such as flayed animal skin which you hang upwind of them and away from where you infiltrate, or bring a female dog that is in heat to the fence so that it distracts them. In addition to this observe light and dark patrols, gate security and the position of external guards.

Activating the enemy emergency protocol

Often the enemy know that there are enemy agents watching them even though they cannot see them. Therefore it is no surprise to them that they are being observed. One trick performed by shinobi of old is to actually set off the alarm on purpose; this was most likely done by teams of shinobi where one agent set off the alarms or created a distraction and the others observed how the camp reacted. For example, setting fires nearby, letting horses out, blowing up vehicles etc., This put the camp into a state of emergency and the observing shinobi were able to identify what the camp protocols are and then plan around them. Of course this is not a good option in times of peace and the enemy are not expecting an attack. Judgment is needed here.

Entry and exit points

If the target has a good gate protocol set up then this will be difficult to bypass; however, before a shinobi mission the agents must identify their entry point and their exit strategy. They also have to decide if they are going to split up or stay together. This will depend on the situation. Chikamatsu-sensei advises splitting up into groups and forming teams that have a goal, such as an assassination squad, a fire squad or distraction team and with each team working in unison to a central goal the enemy will become confused. Remember your entry point will seldom be your exit point; therefore, move in fast, perform the task and escape from another prearranged point.

The pre-attack fire strike

Before moving in on attack, have a diversion attack standing by ready to cause a commotion. This can be a night attack from the south while you attack from the east, or it can be an explosives squad all hitting the compound with hard-fire while the shinobi creeps in from a different direction. The main point here is misdirection. Unleash a heavy assault from one side and attack from the other, but remember, do not always attack from the opposite side. Often a commander being attacked from the left will say "defend the right," so do not be too predictable with your shinobi infiltration route.

Communication

There needs to be communication between HQ and the shinobi team and between the shinobi teams themselves. This can be in many forms, from low-light torches to hand signals and from rope to relay systems.

Low-light torches—Very low-light torches can be used to send signals between team members. Extreme low light will be hard for the enemy to detect unless they happen on it by chance.

Rope system—A shinobi on the edge of an enemy camp can lead a long thin cord backwards for quite some distance. A system can be put in place where a certain amount of tugs on the rope means a specific thing. A shinobi can then silently signal a bigger team to come forward if the coast is clear. Signals such as advance, stop, and retreat can be given.

Relay team—Shinobi sometimes act as a relay team. The main shinobi observing the enemy can pass a report on to another shinobi. That shinobi then can run and pass on that message. This continues until it gets back to the main strike force that is waiting to attack.

Signals with natural elements—Sometimes when the main performer of a shinobi mission has gotten into the enemy compound they will need to signal the other members of the team. To do this they will rustle a branch or throw a small stone back over the wall with a predetermined meaning. This is known as *making wood and stone talk* in the Natori-Ryu school.

Secret signals in instruments—When in a war-zone and it is well known to the enemy that agents are present, then the shinobi outside the camp can use musical instruments to send secret messages to spies that have infiltrated the enemy compound. Imagine that you are in Africa and the steel gates are closed but there are a few hundred men inside the compound. One of them is a planted agent. Playing the track "Light my Fire" by the Doors could be a signal to set fires, or "For Those about to Rock" by AC/DC could be a signal for an explosive. In old Japan this was done using flutes or conch shells. The point is this—the allied force is near the enemy camp, the allies have an agent inside the enemy camp and they are given a command through music or signal to perform a specific deed. Then when the deed is done, such as with a fire or an exposition, other shinobi creep in and set more fires and cause more chaos, allowing the main raid force to attack.

Passwords and security

As seen in the defending list of teachings, an infiltrator knows that there multiple selections of passwords that change every night. To counter this there are a few options.

- Befriend someone of a very low rank and bribe them for the basic passwords.
- Approach someone of low rank and play dumb as if you have forgotten the passwords and ask them to remind you – sweeten the deal with cigarettes and alcohol.
- If it is a temporary compound, infiltrate when the fortification is being built as the passwords are not normally given out until it is finished or if there are passwords it is much easier to get them.
- Become a hired worker for the camp.
- Creep close to the gate house and listen for that days passwords, retreat and then enter.
- Become hired by a high ranking person of the camp, as their servant or aide (this means as a warrior being in a very low and demeaning position) and this way they will guide you in.
- Steal identifying markers from anyone who has been killed around the camp or take out someone to get their identification markers.

Overall, the basic principle is that an infiltrator will watch the routine of the compound and then assess what is needed, where the passwords are given and how many they need. Then they will skirt around the outside, either in plain sight, pretending to be a workman or low level solider and or in secret and pick up those elements.

Light

Light is always an issue for the infiltrator, the following sections discus the area of avoiding light:

Infiltrating with the moon—Only infiltrate when the moon is half dark, moving to fullly dark or approaching half-lit. This means that for half of the period of a lunar month the moon is darker than it is bright, allowing for a darker night.

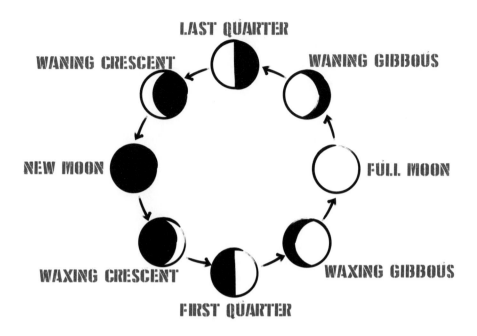

Use the shadows—While it is obvious to say "use the shadows," make sure to use the shadows that fall over the compound wall. In old Japan they used to cut back any trees or forests near castles and camps. This was because it is a prime place for shinobi to infiltrate from or hide in. If there are shadows from nearby trees or external buildings that fall over the compound wall, use that shadow to cover your approach to the wall and then scale the wall from that angle.

Low light torches or sound—Communicate with your team through very low lights or small sounds, such as clicks and wind chimes, this is normally only done in the middle of the night when you have passed the outer guards. Unless directly looking at it, a guard will not see low light and they will ignore small sounds and such things tend not to wake the sleeping.

Infiltrating methods

Actual crossing of a barrier normally consists of going over it, going through it or going under it. All three of which are easy to understand. Climb over, cut through or dig under. Issui-sensei tells us that digging under a wall is a good move, as dogs often dig under fences and walls, so it is nothing new to the enemy but if an infiltrator breaks the wall, it is clearly done by a human. However, modern concrete and foundations will stop this, all will depend on the compound type. The following sections explain the different ways ancient shinobi used to consider their approach for infiltration:

Create a diversion—Create a diversion by shooting in a specific area to bring everyone's attention to that direction. With their attention focused elsewhere there are less "eyes" searching the defenses and more noise to cover movement.

Try to infiltrate in a period of movement—Whenever there is movement in the compound such as a change of guard, the arrival of a visitor, meal times or anything which is a period of movement for those inside, then consider this as a time of infiltration. It is better to get inside when people are moving around instead of when people are still. The only other option for this is when all are asleep and it is the dead of night, but that is also the quietest time making for different difficulties.

Infiltrate during celebration or mourning—When a force has had victory or defeat it is followed by celebration or mourning and exhaustion. This includes general parties or periods of depression. These two emotional extremes leave people in a state of being non-attentive to their tasks, so no matter if they have defeated the allies in battle, when they return to celebrate it is a time to infiltrate. The defeat of an allied army is a highlighted time to use shinobi.

Infiltrate when they move out to attack—The gate is a very strictly guarded area most of the time; however, when the enemy move out to attack, allowing a large force to come out of the compound and through the gate then it is a time when no passwords are used or confusion will occur. They normally open the gate and allow troops to move out *en mass*. Attendants on the gate will then start closing the gates and setting up the security again. It is this time that an infiltrator should carry something through the gate, acting as one of the worker staff.

Infiltrate with heavy weather—When the rain is lashing down, the wind is howling then the guards are inattentive an infiltrator can move in. If the weather makes people wet, cold and miserable, they focus on getting through the watch and less on the environment.

Dressing as the enemy—Make sure to be dressed like the enemy. In old Japan this was called *bakemonojutsu*—the skill of the shape shifter. Dress as the enemy would expect you to be dressed and remember there may be hundreds of them. So an infiltrator will blend in without too many problems in the dark. If you are infiltrating in the dark as a group who are all dressed in the same way, don't rely on using passwords only. Also use identification marks such as headbands or cloth tied to an appendage. That way you can know real friend from foe.

Internal and external layout memorizing

It is essential to fully understand the internals of both a building and an enemy compound. The objective of infiltration is to get deep into the heart of the enemy, to where they sleep and to where they relax and live. This is normally the most, well-guarded area outside of treasure storage. Remember people treasure both gold and their own lives. There are two ways to get internal information on the enemy stronghold:

1. External estimation
2. Internal observation

External estimation—If the compound is well guarded—workers are checked and vetted, door protocol is tight and there is no reasonable pretext for entry—then external estimation has to be used. This requires measuring the outer wall and drawing a diagram or by building a model. If the insides can be seen from a height then also draw and estimate the size of inner buildings. Observe doorways and windows and then try to build a possible layout of the enemy buildings and do not forget to produce a map of the walkways and external paths. Identify where the stairs may be and where rooms end. Sometimes there will be a second team used to simply sit in an observation point and make notes—possibly for weeks on end—until a full understanding of the whole compound and its routine is obtained. This information is passed on to the infiltration team. With the best possible internal map created, memorize it and practice the infiltration.

Internal observation—Internal observation is to either have a third party go into the house or for the agent themselves to get into the house and observe the insides. Fujibayashi-sensei advocates the use of females placed in the service of the house master, either as a maid or as a sex object. In this way she has full reign of the house and the inner bedroom, can stay a prolonged time and even aid on the night of the infiltration by sending signals to the team outside and by opening doors and windows. The second version is to hire locals to go as tradesmen into the house to make repairs, or any form of business which is deemed ok for them to enter, as locals and known to the area this creates less suspicion. They will then make mental notes of the insides. It is of course better to have fully-trained agents do this but it will depend on the situation and the tightness of the security. Another option is to go in to the house yourself under pretext. Issui-sensei tells us that an agent should feign illness, such as sudden diarrhea or heat stroke etc. (but never drunkenness) and to beg help at the front door, manipulating human kindness. At this point the agent should not push to get in the house but just accept water at the door. Then move on. A few days later the agent "returns" with gifts and is looking well. At this point, unless it is a very strictly controlled military compound, then the agent will be allowed inside to give gifts of thanks. This gives the agent the opportunity to memorize the internals, such as layout and door and window types and then to leave with the information needed to infiltrate later that night.

Dry runs

With all the information collated from both inside people and external observation, chalk out and mock up the building internals. With this model in place, run through the infiltration many times, team movement, infiltration points and exit strategy, when and where to divide the team and time the process. Remember, the shinobi way is to get in quick, perform the task and be gone very quickly but also quietly, use the lightest possible plan with the least amount of problem points.

A cord to lead you out

Attach a thin cord to the entry point at the main fence, or to a post when you move into a larger house. In the dark, this acts as a way back to the entrance point with speed, just in case of emergency. Remember, always have an exit planned beforehand but in an attack try to use a different exit point from your entry point. Otherwise, you may have to double back through the enemy, but in a quiet infiltration it is acceptable to come back out the way you came in as no one should know that you have been there. Therefore, in an emergency this cord will get you back out of an unfamiliar house and with speed if needed.

Vehicle Movement

When moving in vehicles, there are certain points to keep in mind and ways to think as a team. Much of it is basic and just requires good protocol and training. The following sections are a basic overview:

Keep the principle in the center

When driving in convoy, keep the principle vehicle in the center of the convoy and protect it. Have the fastest vehicles at the front, such as motorcycles, etc., to act as scouts. This is no different from movement in a samurai army, fast scouts go to the front, the command is in the center and equipment goes to the rear; however, the equipment must have protection. Here we are talking about a quick moving pack of vehicles and most likely will carry their own kit. Moving up to the larger level would be more in line with full scale samurai warfare.

Plan the route in advance

Plan your route in advance, picking the least amount of ambush points which also allows for the most amount of movement and freedom to escape a situation. Make sure to have an alternative or emergency route and way points for if you become split up and maintain communication between vehicles along with call names.

Communication with HQ

If a headquarters has been established, make sure that they are aware of the planned routes and emergency protocol of the vehicle group. Also the general times that way points will be reached and the ETA of the final arrival. This does however open up the possibility of the routes being open to enemy eyes if agents have been planted or for bribes to take place inside of HQ.

Leapfrogging

Leap frogging is to have the lead car block off an upcoming road or junction.

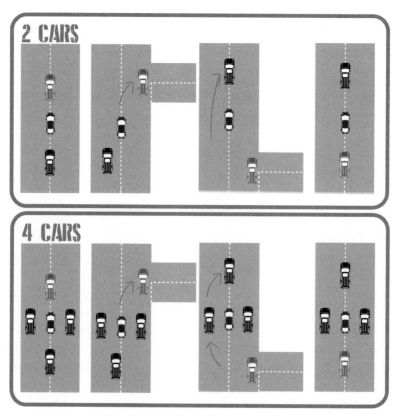

Vectors courtesy of Vecteezy.com.

This stops the traffic from crossing the path of the principle vehicle. When the principle vehicle has gone past this junction or possible danger point, another vehicle moves up to the position of front vehicle. The vehicle that is back at the cross roads waits for the principle car to pass and then follows on directly behind, making that vehicle the rear protection. This happens over and over again at each possible danger point or junction. With more than two cars, this simply changes to a rotation method where the car to the side will move up.

Boxing in

When you wish to bring a car to a standstill "box it in" by putting a car to each of the four sides of it, then in unison slow down and decelerate until all cars come to a stop. You can also use this to protect the principle car in a convoy which will keep enemy cars from getting close to either the command or someone of worth. Again this is done with personal protection, bodyguards will do the same by boxing in their principle and forcing others to move out of the way.

Vectors courtesy of Vecteezy.com.

Snatch and Grab

"Snatch and grab" is to capture targets as hostages to be interrogated or ransomed. The main difference here is that with a *kill team*, they only need an exit strategy for themselves; however, with a *snatch and grab* they need to take an unwilling person with them and therefore, the exit strategy needs to be revised.

Samurai armor from the Natori-Ryu encyclopedia,
found in *The Book of Samurai* Series.

CHAPTER 3

In the Open

*t*he true test of a security team or agent is being in enemy territory. It is less dangerous to work in public places where law and order are in effect, but often security teams or agents work inside of hostile and enemy territory. This means that what they do is illegal—if there are laws in place in the area beyond rule by strength and power—and they will have to move either covertly or overtly. Covertly, can be moving without being seen, hiding from the enemy or can mean disguised as a local. Overtly means to be in full view in hostile territory but to show a strength of arms and to move in a hostile manner.

In Enemy Territory

When entering enemy territory—no matter if it is large or small—a team can enter into that territory in one of four main ways, two covert ways and two overt ways:

Covert Option 1

The first is to stay out of sight totally, to have an entry point and an exit point or evacuation strategy, to move through in total stealth, perform the task at hand and then exit by never being seen.

Covert Option 2

The second is to have a cover story in place so that there is a reason why armed personnel in a vehicle are moving through the country. An example of this type of cover story is that the team is working for an NGO and have been tasked with making a report on the impact of charity on a developing area and to establish where the impact will have most benefit. Private military units may use this type of story as a cover to cross over dangerous areas and to move through checkpoints. This also allows for better relationships with regional warlords as they will wish to treat the team well to try to sway them to make the decision to give the charity to their domain (of course the warlord woiuld then confiscate the aid). In this manner teams can move under a pretext.

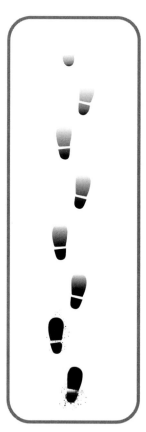

The term low footprint means to leave littlo to no ovidonco of infiltration.

Overt Option 1

The first overt method is defensive. That means to have hard-skinned vehicles, heavy firepower and to move in convoy, taking on a "*do not mess with us and we will not mess with you*" approach. A show of power but without any hostile intent but with the attitude of you clearly "mean business."

Overt Option 2

The second overt method is aggressive. To *shoot first and ask no questions later.* When entering a village/town in what is well known to be hostile areas, the convoy will open fire at the first people it sees no matter who they are, be it check-point, soldier or civilian. The message is clear: *"get back and stay down."* The people of the village/town will hide and the convoy moves through each area like this.

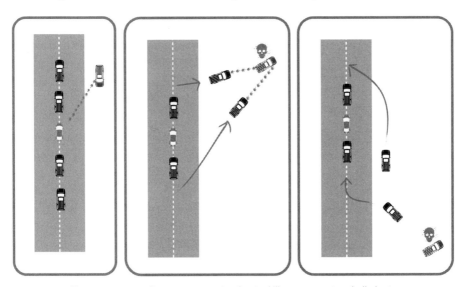

The enemy opens fire on a convoy, two hunter-killers move out and eliminate them and then return to the line. Vectors courtesy of Vecteezy.com.

The next element is the hunter-killer tactic. If the convoy is attacked, some of the vehicles will break off and pursue the people or vehicles who have made the assault, the rest of the convoy go into heavy defensive mode. The two hunter-killer vehicles will not stop in their pursuit of the hostile enemy until they have killed them. The word will then spread that attacking teams only leave corpses behind.

Noise discipline—equipment

Each agent is responsible for their own noise reduction by securing the gear on their bodies in a way that prevents it from rattling, sloshing, clinking, etc. To check this, jump up and down on the spot to see what parts of your equipment makes noise. Anything that is making a noise should be tapped, strapped or tied down. Continue this test until all elements have stopped making noise.

The shinobi of old also performed noise reduction. They would keep equipment in leather bags that they could roll up tight to stop things jangling and only got them out when they were at their destination. It is important to remember the difference between *shinobi no mono*—a ninja who is trained to do a specific task and the idea of *shinobi-iru* which means to enter in stealth. For example, when using horses at night to enter enemy territory in stealth, their hooves would be filled with wet paper and then covered in straw to dampen the sound, their mouth bits would be wrapped in cloth to stop them jangling and their tongues would be tied up to stop them neighing. Likewise, samurai armor would be tied up to stop any clanking, the underside of plates would have leather attached to stop any clinking and at times, they would take their *kimono* out from below their armor tassets, fold it upwards and tug it into their belts, this stopped the tasset protection plates from jumping about (see image below for part names).

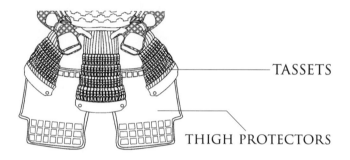

TASSETS

THIGH PROTECTORS

Basically, noise reduction on equipment is the individual's responsibility and it will change depending on the equipment used.

Checkpoints

Checkpoints are barriers set up along roads and pathways. In their most structured form they are airport passport control, port authorities, boarder checkpoints; in their most basic form they are road blockages by gangs.

Checkpoints are established for four main reasons:

1. Security of an area.
2. To control traffic and goods.
3. For political power.
4. To take money.

Checkpoints are an issue for security teams as they can be a source of problems: they can be a waste of time, they can cost money to get through and there is a potential for violence. However, there are ways to get through checkpoints effectively.

Bypassing checkpoints

There are multiple ways to get past checkpoints. The most obvious is to go around them; however, this can take time and fuel, could lead to an ambush or into dangerous or difficult terrain. The main rule is to approach a checkpoint with care and observe the situation, have tight protocols and command words in place and never just ride into a checkpoint unprepared. The following are four basic ways to get through a checkpoint.

Rapport—Build rapport with the security guards—talk to them, and engage them with politeness and respect. If one is wearing a sports shirt, talk about their favorite team, offer them food or drink, or engage in nice, relaxed conversation until they are bored and let you pass.

Attack on approach—When you have identified a checkpoint, prepare and arm yourselves. Start shooting as you approach and keep the fire heavy—guards will normally scatter out of the way. Make sure to keep shooting as you move through. Build a reputation for eliminating those who stand in your team's way so that fear grips them first.

Command word kill—A team should have various passwords and signs in place for when conversation at a checkpoint is going badly. If the team captain feels that the situation will escalate into violence (probably a fire fight), the team will move to kill on the captain's command. For example, if a debate is getting heated, and the team knows this, the captain may say, "I am going to get out of my car slowly so we can talk about this." The captain will then start to show very passive movement while opening the door. At this point, the rest of the team shoots the guards while the guards are focused on the captain's fake, passive exit from the car. Each team should create their own selection of passwords and signs to be used in various situations.

The distraction—There are times when a distraction will work. It is good practice to keep a roll of $1 bills in all doors of the car. If the situation demands it, take the elastic band off the bills and toss them out of the car, making sure they spread out.

If the guards are badly trained, they will scramble about for the money and you can drive off. They may take a few pot shots, so be aware of your vehicle's rear defenses.

Shinobi and samurai check points

Remembering that Japan was under military rule for the best part of 1,000 years. Checkpoints were nothing new for the samurai and shinobi. Checkpoints were set up along commonly-used routes and were used for the same four principles described above:

1. Security—used in towns and cities to check movement.
2. To control the local populations.
3. To cause issues when new factions rose to power.
4. To tax goods.

The samurai and shinobi also had various ways to bypass checkpoints.

As a messenger and servant—The samurai, if on a mission as a messenger, would sometimes be allowed to pass, even though they were an enemy as they would carry messages between both lords who were at war. In this case, shinobi agents were often attached to those samurai to act as servants so that they could break off from the samurai and find their contact in the area and bring back a secret report. During these operation both the samurai messenger and the shinobi had ways to carry secret notes. A samurai would keep a note in the ventilation hole at the top of his helmet while a shinobi dressed as a peasant would cut the message up and weave it into cords of their hat, stich it into their underwear or carry it in a hidden compartment in a religious figurine. Shinobi often used festivals and pilgrimage routes to enter enemy areas.

To bypass a check point—If it was too difficult to get through a checkpoint or security was increased, the shinobi would follow the "teachings of foxes and wolves"—avoid human contact as an animal would. This means journeying miles out of your way, in all-weather, to get around check points. This could include cliff face climbs, river crossings, long distance travel and various other things. However, it should be remembered that at some times in old Japan to avoid a checkpoint meant instant death penalty, so it was risky business. Another way to do this was to use the skill of *kyodo,* which means to ask locals (oftentimes through bribes) to find pathways over the mountains.

The following is a collection of quotes from original ninja manuals about the art of bypassing checkpoints.

PRIMARY EVIDENCE

When you come across a checkpoint in the enemy's province, one which inspects both outgoing and incoming traffic, do not try to pass through it by various means. You should do as foxes and wolves do and try to find a bypass.
—*True Path of the Ninja* (1681)

In cases concerning checkpoints, you should be aware of the following things: disguise yourself as a courier, beggar or outcast when passing through a check-point. If there is a Shinto service or festival, there will be some wild merrymaking, where you can become mixed in with others and pass through the checkpoint. It is difficult for them to check everyone closely on such an occasion so you should take advantage of such a festival if you can.
—*Secret Traditions of the Shinobi* (16th and 17th century)

Those who guard checkpoints should not be weak of mind in anyway. If someone suspicious comes through, they should be stopped and thoroughly checked. Those who do the job of shinobi and togiki are people of wit and thus are excellent at deceiving people.
—*Samurai and Ninja* (from Ogasawara 17th century)

If you need to have the person remain in the province—as when the group comes back, the number of people is to be checked [at the checkpoint]—then you should take the following measures: have one person feign to be ill and pretend to die of that illness, then bury him. When night comes, dig him out and refill the ground so the spy can stay in that province without being noticed. If the body is to be cremated, then you should kill someone from the [enemy] province and replace your spy with this dead body before it is cremated.

—*Iga and Koka Ninja Skills* (17th century)

Water

If you have ever enjoyed camping and mountaineering in the wild, you know the danger that even the smallest river can pose. Rivers are a natural boundary. While a slow river may be easy to swim across in summer, in cold weather the slightest current will prevent most people from crossing by swimming alone. Rivers are formed of multiple parts including source, upper course, middle course, lower course, rapids, riffles, pools and runs—there are sections that can easily sweep you away or pull you under. Further dangers include fallen trees (which often become a network of dangerous spikes), steep cliff embankments (which cannot be climbed, and of course waterfalls (where even the smallest drop can bring great injury or death).

A full military force, be it modern or ancient, relies on the engineering corps to get them across rivers; however shinobi and single operators rely on themselves or a few teammates. The following sections identify some skills on dealing with rivers when not supported by a bridge-building unit.

Crossing rivers

Historical shinobi scrolls and modern survival training manuals offer the same techniques for crossing rivers showing that nothing has really changed on the subject for the soldier that operates forward of an army. Remembering that single operators and shinobi must value safety, we also have to consider that they are the troops that push well beyond safe areas, therefore modern safety guides do not apply to them. In fact, not only are they crossing violent rivers, they are doing so in enemy territory. The following methods are for team crossing.

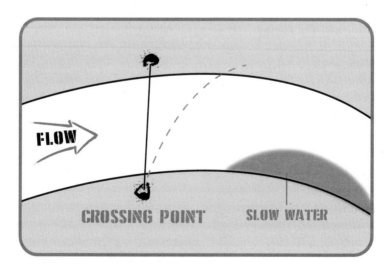

Team river crossing: step 1—If possible find a bend in the river, one that angles back towards you as shown in the image on the previous page. As the river runs into the bend, the force of the flow will push the team onto the opposite bank. If there are problems it will naturally send a member closer to the opposite side as they are swept around the bend. Furthermore, on the opposite side of a river bend the water is slower, offering a safe point from which to move in and help. Lastly, identify if there are anchor points in the area of the crossing. If not you will have to form temporary ones.

Team river crossing: step 2—The strongest swimmer on the team should strip naked or to their underwear—so their clothes remain dry and can be passed over later—and attach a cord to their waist (either tied on or attached to a belt). The cord should be thin and light, the opposite end held by those who remain on the bank. This means that one end of the cord is attached to the swimmer and the other end is attached to a thicker rope (which will become the bridge). To attach two ropes of unequal thickness together use a sheet bend as seen at right.

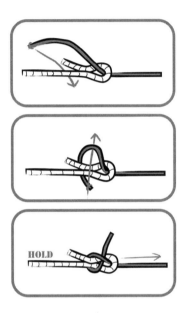

The swimmer then crosses. Once on the other side the swimmer pulls the cord across until they have the thicker rope and both ends are attached to anchor points.

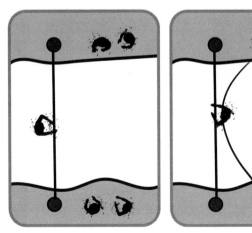

The image on the left shows a single line with no safety attached to the person crossing, this is simple to perform. The image on the right shows a second thinner line used as a safety line—with this version do not allow the person crossing to tie the line directly to them, instead have it pass through their belt or through a carabiner. The reason for this is that both ends have to stay on their respective shores so that the line can be used for the transport of goods across.

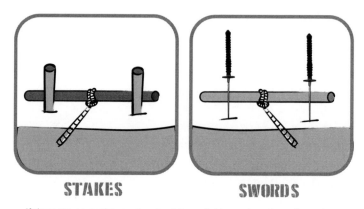

STAKES   SWORDS

If there are no anchor or strong points available, such as trees, heavy logs, rocks, etc., then temporary strong points need to be created. This can be done by putting stakes in the ground and then having a branch behind them. This can be done with swords, machetes, and a rifle or any form of strong cross bar.

Team river crossing: step 3—When all but one of the team is across, the last member unties the main rope and attaches it to themselves, the rest of the team helps pull them across.; when complete all will be across. The only other element to consider is equipment transport.

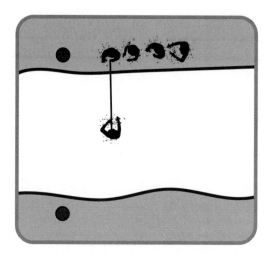

Equipment transport

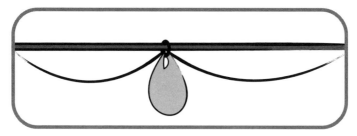

An iron ring looped over a rope with cord used to pull equipment backwards and forwards.

To pass equipment across a river, take a circlet with you. This can be a premade iron circle, a rope circle (known as a strop), a short piece of rope or a carabiner. This is hooped onto the secured line before it is tied off to the anchor points. Remember that the people on each river bank need to have one end each. When this setup is complete, tie kit directly on to the ring and transport the equipment over the river by pulling the ring back and forth with a line.

Linked river crossing

Another way to cross a river was to link each troop member together. In old Japan the people used their *sageo* sword cords and tied them to the back of each person. This can also be done with short ropes. The strength of the whole team would keep everyone together and brace against anyone losing their footing. In addition to rivers, this was also done at night, in dark areas and in heavy weather where visibility is low.

Floating aides

The shinobi had forms of floating aids such as jackets, water seats, rafts, buoyancy bags, etc. The subject is quite a large one, and there are many variations, from spear rafts all the way to bridges. The shinobi would often travel down rivers using these floating devices to get them to their destination quicker. Remember, a shinobi is not in the wilderness "surviving." The shinobi is out there infiltrating the enemy. Often the safest option is not the option they tend to take. Therefore, swimming in rivers is a must for a shinobi. This would be done with buoyancy, but it would have to be done over great distances and in extreme weather.

Movement in rivers and water

A shinobi should not be seen to disturb the water, nor make a sound in it. There are various ways to perform silent water movement; however, with all elements of silent movement, slowness equals quietness.

The drawing out step—The Japanese have a step called *nukiashi*. This is to draw the foot out of the water vertically with the toes tipping downwards. The aim is to stop the sloshing sound when wading through water. Pull the foot up vertically and then move it forward slightly and place it back in the water, toes down. Next pull the rear foot up in the same manner and move forward again. Imagine this as a knife point going in and out of the water.

Move with the flow of water—When creeping up on an enemy camp, come from upstream and move downstream. This allows the water to flow around you as you will be travelling with the water and not against it. If you travel against the water then you will create a sucking sound as you fight to step forward. Therefore, infiltrate a camp from upstream.

Camouflage in the water—In war, the rivers will have flotsam in them, things that have been cast to the side, old containers, the dead, building materials, etc. One trick used by Natori-Ryu is to make a spy hole in a used rice container and place it over the head and then enter the water. The shinobi then floats past the camp with the spy hole turned towards the camp so that they can observe the camp structure and other elements. It would be common to see debris in the water and this would not cause suspicion as long as it floats naturally.

Hiding in the shallows—If people are approaching, move to the edge of a river where the reeds overhand or where you can tuck your body into the bank. Gather foliage around you and keep only your eyes and nose above the water. There should be very little showing of your head and you should be well hidden in the foliage.

Snorkeling—The shinobi of old used a reed or bamboo pipe or a cut-down scabbard, or the scabbard of a short sword as a snorkel. They would either swim across a moat and dive and surface for air briefly as they moved across the water or they would use their sword and embed it in the river bed, holding the handle and breathing through the pipe/scabbard while the enemy passed. There is a myth that this is not possible because of the

length of the scabbard; however, the swords they used were either short swords (so the scabbards were short) or they are cut down katana scabbards or even short pipes of bamboo. The myth of the scabbard being too long is a misunderstanding of the historical documentation. Medieval sources do discuss a shorter snorkel.

Commando canoe

The shinobi made use of shallow-draft boats to move along rivers and moats. These were cleverly created so that they could be dismantled and reassembled on a mission with an outer skin of leather, or they were a series of boxes with two bow shaped ends, and when all were fixed together they formed a canoe.

Marshland

Marshland is often the least guarded territory as it forms a natural defense; therefore the shinobi often cross it to infiltrate. There are various ways of crossing marshland depending on the extent of the marsh.

The spear butt cross bar—Attach a small bar of wood to the bottom of your spear perpendicular to the shaft, then use the spear in both hands and make it become a "third leg." The bar does not sink in a light marsh and this gives extra stability allowing you to move in a tripod motion with the bar stopping the spear from sinking too far.

Marsh shoes—Flat boards of wood larger than the feet are strapped on like sandals. In light marshes these can allow a person to walk over the grassy and wet ground (very much like snow shoes).

Two board shuffle—If the marsh is deep and muddy, construct two boards made of wicker. Place one on the ground and step on it. Next, place the other one ahead. Step onto the next board and then retrieve the one you just left. Keep doing this in unison, one board after the other, until the marsh is crossed.

Hostile Terrain

One larger element that is not discussed here is survival in the wilderness. The restrictions on length mean that this element has to be brief; however, wilderness survival, extreme camping and travel, shelter building, fire starting and hunting are all covered in depth in many survival books and such information is readily available. However, do not underestimate the importance of survival and travel in open areas, a topic which you should study as a foundation to the skills in this book.

Hostile Engagement

W hile a part of being an infiltrator is obviously about staying out of sight, blending in with others or surviving in harsh conditions, it is also about engagement with the enemy and often, the final phase of an infiltration will be engagement and death. This can happen in both urban and wilderness areas. The following sections are an overview of how to interact with an enemy and how to react or act in certain situations.

Urban Movement

Urban movement is movement within an urban setting, such as buildings, towns, villages, cities, indusial areas, etc. This requires a much higher level of understanding of three dimensional awareness. Buildings are multi-storey, windows give vantage points, rooms become a complex maze and therefore you must always be assessing threats from all high points and around corners.

Three-dimensional environments require three dimensional observation. An urban landscape means that you are threatened from multiple levels and multiple angles. Assign various team members tasks and directions, but all should stay alert with a three-dimensional mind-set.

Share Group Responsibility

Make sure that people have basic roles such as defending the rear, observing the flanks, both upwards and on ground level, and have someone focused to the front. While all troops should maintain three dimensional awareness, have each member to cover a basic sector.

Map Memorizing

Before moving into an area, excellent reconnaissance must be done or a map of the area attained. It is essential to fully understand a map of the area and the locations in a city or urban area—from an enemy compound to a full city center, know the directions of roads and pathways, locations of buildings, fully understand the street system and best exit strategy, enemy locations, enemy routine in connection to the map and the best routes for your incursion and extraction. This of course has to be done by memory so that you can move in haste, alternatively have technology that can guide you unless it does not fit well with your pretext if undercover.

Moving Up to Junctions

Moving up to a junction means that the team is open to attack from the side. One member or group, be it in a vehicle or in a ground team, moves up to the road junction, left, right or from both directions and covers the road until the team has moved past the threat.

Crossing Difficult Points

To cross a road or difficult point such as a bottleneck or place where it is easy to be shot at, send one member across quickly. They will then act as lookout. The rest of the team should cross at different points so that it is not easy for the enemy to open fire on the same point if the team crossed in a single file. The last person to cross should do so at an unexpected place and cover the rear. The team should not be scattered, but be within proximity to each other.

1. First person crosses and acts as defense.
2. The team quickly crosses at slightly different locations.
3. The last person moves and covers the rear.
4. Team moves on.

With a larger force, the force is broken up into four sections:

1. Scouts.
2. Forward defense.
3. Main unit.
4. Rear defense.

When approaching a dangerous area, the scouts move ahead and signal back. However, in case they missed any threat, a smaller but substantial forward group should cross over and take up an aggressive position but leave enough space for the main force to form behind them. The main force crosses and forms up behind the forward defense. Next, the rear protection group crosses and pays attention to the rear at all times. They then rejoin the group and all move off with the scouts returning to normal duty. Finally, the force reforms its marching order.

Seeing Beyond a Door

To see if someone is to the side of the door, move up to the wall and place your face flat against it, eyes towards the door. This will give you a slim angle to see the area just behind the doorway. In this situation the door must be open. One person moves up to the wall and takes up this position. When they confirm no one is to the side of the door, the rest of the team enter the door with normal checks. The person at the wall then becomes rear-guard. The skill of looking through the door at an angle is based on the teachings of Arisawa, a samurai of the 17th century and is based on sliding doors. This only works on Western doors by looking from the side with the hinges towards an open door.

Approaching a Corner

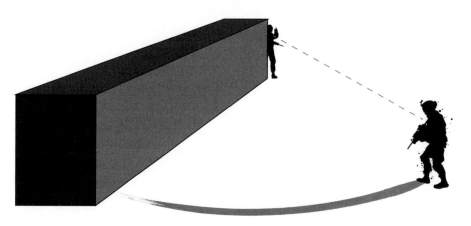

Always approach corners with caution—never just walk up and around them. Give them some space and allow yourself to see if anyone is around the corner. This can be called "slicing the pie" which means to move out away from the wall first and then move towards the corner, giving you line of sight with an enemy hiding behind the wall. If this is done in extremely hostile territory with weapons primed and ready, move around slowly. The first thing you should see if the enemy is there is their elbow as they hold the weapon ready. Remember, if they have their backs to the wall waiting for you, their right elbow will be out. If they are facing the wall waiting for you, their left elbow will be out. Shoot this elbow/arm first and then move with speed and shoot their body. This is for when you move up to a corner on *your* left, if the corner is on *your* right, the above is reversed. If you are approaching a corner on your right, you can use the skill of change arms, which means to use your left hand as the trigger hand and your right hand as the support so that your own elbow profile is lessened. This is based on you being right handed, left handed people will do the reverse.

Proactive Shooting

Rules of Engagement (ROE) and Use of Force (UOF) guidelines for the military outline how one should conduct themselves in times if violence, both at war and at home; however, for the shinobi these rules did not exist and for the single operator working outside of military command, or even Special Forces working clandestinely, these rules are often ignored or not even considered. For the agent deep in enemy territory there is no waiting for the enemy to shoot first, one should simply engage in proactive shooting. Bearing in mind there are times not to shoot, the main focus is, if threatened, start shooting. Engage the enemy before they engage you; create a situation where they are at a disadvantage and you are one step ahead. Waiting to be shot at puts the team behind the curve. Be aware of everythng around you—be aware of the enemy before they are aware of you, and take them down as quickly as possible. In developing countries where crime is rife, it is often a case of shoot to kill and shoot first. Questions are seldom asked at any time.

Shoot on Sight

If walking alone at night in violent territory where murder and crime is at a high level, shoot on sight. It is standard practice for some security personnel who have to stay in such areas to shoot anyone who approaches them at night, no matter what for. In truth, in such areas and not being a local, it is obvious that this is a robbery or a kidnapping. Therefore, upon the first words they utter, draw and shoot to kill. Any others will scatter at this if it's a robbery or opportunity kidnapping. Old Japan was also dangerous at night. Issui-sensei talks of this skill for the samurai in the following quote.

PRIMARY EVIDENCE

夜盗賊辻切取捌之事
Yoru Tozoku Tsujigiri Torisabaki no Koto
Dealing with thieves and roadside killers at night

When travelling or venturing long distances, at certain places at night, you may be attacked by roadside killers, highwaymen and the like. When in such a place, move silently and with care and do not become flustered. If someone approaches you to steal gold and silver, kill them immediately and leave it at that. If there are more than just one then simply kill one of them and the rest will flee, remember that the mind of a thief is the mind of a coward.
—*The Book of Samurai series (17th century)*

Enemy Contact

While moving in an urban environment or in the wilderness you will inevitably come into contact with the enemy. When moving through enemy territory be ready. The first thing to do when seeing them is call "enemy contact."

Call contact

Upon viewing the enemy, call out "contact left," "contact right," "contact ahead," "contact to the rear," etc. Terminology will depend on the team. When it is called, the team will focus and fire in that direction, with controlled bursts. If the enemy are ahead of the curve then the skill of magazine dumping can be used. One member will open in rapid fire to force the heads of the enemy down while the rest of the team then take the initiative. Be aware of second contacts and ambushes.

Adopt a formation

Often teams will move in formation, adopting a specific formation on contact. This again may depend on the team and their preferred system. But in general, get down lower, have rear observation by at least one member and the rest of the team will then decide to advance or retreat.

Advance or retreat

The team will have to advance or retreat at this point. To do this they will move in sections or small groups. One group will move, the others will fire, then the group that moves will take over and fire and allow the other groups to move up. The system will depend on the amount of groups. Some may peel left, peel right, move up left, move up right, move up the center, etc. There are many combinations. The main point is to have specific groups and to take turns moving and firing. Be aware not to cross through each other's arc of fire and make sure to have at least one team shooting at all times with controlled and directed bursts. This is a rotation of shots from each team to allow movement. In old Japan, with muskets, this rotation of shots was called *tatami-uchi*—rotating fire

Vehicles

When the enemy strikes when you are in a vehicle, unless it is a specially designed vehicle that is hard skinned and can survive a sustained assault, you will probably be killed. There are only a few places that offer resistance against fired rounds. These are:

- The front wheels
- The rear wheels
- The engine block

You must try to position yourself so that any of the above three are between yourself and the shooter. If the vehicle comes under fire from the right you must exit to the left and vice versa. Even if the vehicle is soft skinned you can still prep it for action. Secure smoke grenades to all four doors and line any spare bullet proof vests up against the sides. The use of the bullet proof vest is obvious and helps stop the first rounds, the smoke is there to help you exit the car. For example, on a call "contact right" the people on the right side of the car "pop" the smoke and throw it out of the right window, between the shooters and the car. The people on the left open the doors and get out. They then take up position behind each wheel and the engine block. The basic idea is to put a smoke screen between the shooter and the vehicle and to exit to the opposite side and then take up position. If your vehicle is beyond repair, take out the shooters and take theirs.

Vectors courtesy of Vecteezy.com.

Ambushes

Ambushes are one of the oldest forms of unified warfare in history, ancient man used to ambush larger animals when hunting by running them into specific areas with traps, or into dead drops or confined areas where they could be killed. Ambushes can be very large; for example, Germanic tribes ambushed and destroyed a massive Roman Army at the Battle of the Teutoburg Forest, but ambushes can also be very small. When the British diplomat A.B. Mitford was moving through a Japanese town in the 1850s, he was ambushed by two ronin, even though he had a massive bodyguard. The assassination attempt was unsuccessful but the two ronin did manage to injure many men in the fray as the guards had no time to prepare and such a large force could do nothing in the confined area.

The basic ambush

The concept of the ambush is to wait in hiding for the enemy and hit a point where they have restricted movement. Normally the ambushers have a height advantage and pin down their opponents when they are not in formation and often moving in lines. Whenever you are on the move, any point that cannot be seen along the route or where it is thin and rises to one or more sides is a possible ambush site. This changes depending on the size of the force. A massive army can be ambushed in a valley, but the same valley would be too big to ambush a single shinobi. Therefore the ambush position is relative to the size of the force.

Ambush on a bend

When setting up an ambush against a vehicle, consider that the vehicle has to slow down at a bend. To take advantage of this, set up troops at the point where the car decelerates to its slowest speed. Also position troops at the bend where they have a clear line of sight directly onto the approaching car. This creates two firing lines onto the target vehicle when it is at its slowest point.

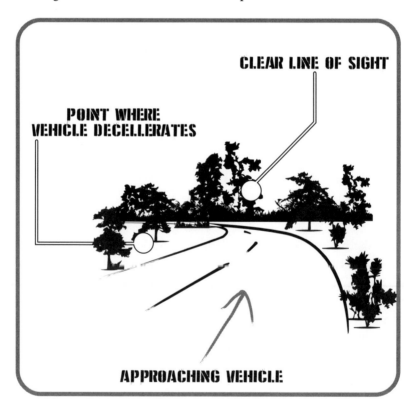

The bait team

Often a bait team is used to urge a force to chase them. This is done because when chasing an enemy both formation and preparedness drop. The bait team lure the enemy into a choke point and others wait to take them out from a vantage point.

Caltrop ambush

At nighttime, send a bait team and have the enemy pursue them. The bait team will run into a position along a road where an ambush is in wait. After the bait team have past, caltrops are thrown down in vast quantities across the whole road. When the enemy run across the caltrops the ambush troops fire at the injured personnel.

The fake forest

Ancient scrolls tell us that one skill of the samurai was to cut down a coppice of trees and take those trees to an ambush point to create a fake woods to hide troops. This meant that the trees could be dropped and troops could run out. Shinobi of old used to observe the distance between the ground and the first branches of trees; if this was too short it was a fake forest.

The fake ambush

Sometimes just the hint of an ambush will force troops to stop or make them change direction. This is used to create more time or to change their route. This can be done by the use of dummies set up as troops and the positioning of false flags. At night torches can be put on a hillside or musket fuses can be hung from trees, all of which can make it appear that an ambush is imminent. However, shinobi teachings tell us that a real ambush should not be seen; therefore if it seems too obvious that troops are there then it is probably a fake ambush.

Defense against Ambush

There are various ways that a single operator, a security team and an army can defend against ambushes. A single operator can move independently; a full army is often given very few choices. The following sections show how to identify and avoid ambushes.

Moving alone

If moving as a single operator, do not take the direct route along well-used roads. Go across country and take the hard route all of the time. This makes for a much longer journey but you will come out at the other end without encountering ambushes. As long as your route is not known, no one will set up ambushes in out of the way places where there is no route. However, if time is of the essence, this cannot be done. Then you must assess risk versus time.

Scout ahead

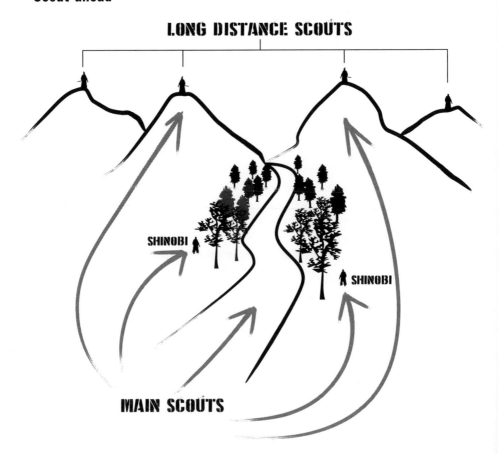

When moving as a large team or full force, use scouts of various types to move ahead of the main body of troops.

- **Main scouts**—these move up the same main route the full force will. An ambush will not give itself away for only a handful of people when the intended target is the full force.
- **Long distance scouts**—these move to tops of mountains and hills in the area and act as the eyes of the army over long distances. They should resemble busy worker bees constantly moving back and forth, coming on and off duty, always "buzzing" around the externals of a force. Shinobi can perform this task.
- **Shinobi scouts**—these small bands of scouts or individuals move around the area ahead but off the roads. They check nearby hilltops, caves, woodlands and crevasses for any ambushes. They move in and around the main route checking off-road along the force's path.

Approaching a bend

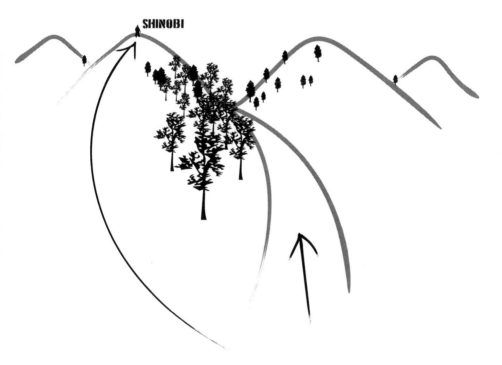

When approaching a bend where there is no visibility around the corner, send one member of the team onto higher ground and come down on the bend from above and behind any possible ambush. If all is clear, the scout drops down onto the bend itself and comes back towards the main force giving the all clear signal.

Observe birds and other wildlife

Old shinobi scrolls constantly mention that an agent should be familiar with the patterns of wildlife and animal behavior. Observe all animals especially the routines of birds. If a flock of birds quickly flies from a tree it is often because something is on the move. If your vantage point is high enough you can see the path of the enemy by watching the birds as they become disturbed in sequence.

If it is an ambush then the birds will have resettled after a while and a scout may not see them take flight; however they will not resettle in trees that contain troops. Therefore, if birds keep avoiding an area of bushland, scrub or trees and their normal flight behavior diverts and changes when they approach a possible ambush area, it is possibly because troops are secretly stationed there. So keep your eyes on the sky and observe the way the birds behave. The reversal of this is knowing that some birds, those used to habitation, will actually flock to humans to find food; therefore, be aware of this possibility. However, this seldom happens in the wild. Other animals may also run out of wooded areas as the enemy moves through, or if your own troops startle wildlife and it flees into a wooded area, but then the animal becomes confused, stops and dashes to the side, away from its intended path, know that it has spotted a danger in that woods, such as troops in ambush and it has tried to find an escape with no people upon it. In short, always observe animal behavior in the wild.

Observe grass from a height

If the area to either side of a possible ambush site is grassy (tall enough to cover a person who is crouching), then send a scout to a height and have them observe the grasslands. If troops are there, trails will still be seen in the grass where people have moved through. Historically the ninja were also known by the names *kusu* and *shimba* which connoted "hiding in grass" and shinobi or shinobi-like troops were used in ambushes.

Above all, shinobi try to avoid contact with the enemy. It is the position of the shinobi to watch the enemy but stay hidden from enemy eyes. Therefore, contact with the enemy is normally only undetaken in emergency situations. If contact is planned it is normally done in disguise or if violent it is an assassination or ambush, the darker side of warfare.

Following the Horrific Path

The samurai-shinobi, Issui-sensei writes in his ancient scrolls, must get used to the foul stench of blood and bile, that they must become familiar with blood-work and violence. He advises the witnessing of various executions in person so that a samurai can steel themselves against blood-weakness. He continues in another section of his scrolls saying that when a samurai performs great deeds, the honor must be attributed to his lord's grace, or if a good move is made behind the political scenes, then it should be said it was the lord's choice. Equally he says when dark deeds are performed for the good of the clan then those deeds should be attributed to the samurai doing them, even if they are the orders of the lord. In his famous scroll the Shoninki (*True Path of the Ninja*), he states clearly that the way of the shinobi is a "horrific path." The world misunderstands samurai honor, the code that they used and how a samurai interacts with the task of shinobi. The samurai code of honor known as *bushido* was not quite how the world imagines it. Honor was found in being the best, in being above others, in domination and in deeds of blood in the name of the clan. Of course the samurai were human and one of their primary aims was to bring about peace, but it was to bring peace at the edge of a sword. The real samurai of history were violent and bloodthirsty. They put heads on spikes, peeled back the faces of the dead, killed civilians, destroyed farms; they did all this in the name of the their lord. But the shinobi went a step beyond, going further than even samurai would go. Shinobi took part in murder, lies, deceit, scandal, disguise, propaganda, sex, slavery, the killing of innocent bystanders, robbery and all the deeds at the depths of human society. They were the dark side of the samurai "coin," not the antithesis of the samurai themselves.

Thief or Shinobi?

What is the difference between the shinobi and the robber-thief? The answer lies in the *intent* in which they practiced their skills. In reality, they would look almost the same; their skills would have been similar but their target result would be different. The shinobi stressed over and over again that they were not thieves—they were shinobi. But people often mix them up, which tells us that they probably did actually mix and many shinobi most likely also turned out to be thieves. Also, consider the divide between those samurai who, in loyal service agreed to undertake the role of shinobi, versus those people who are thieves by profession who agreed to undertake the role of shinobi. Both of them performed this function for a lord but had different upbringings and outlooks on life. The line between the two are difficult to separate; however, consider that a loyal shinobi retainer performs these acts to further the lord's will and his clan, while the employed external shinobi performs those deeds for financial reward. The thief performs the same deeds for instant financial gratification and sexual exploits. One theme in Edo-period art is the idea of the sneak thief and rape—the killing of a home's occupants and the defilement of women. These individuals are often dressed as the archetypal ninja.

Remember that the idea of shinobi is an umbrella term. It is a word that represents a wide variety of backgrounds and levels in society, the same as "black ops" can mean a wide variety of things. It can mean that you use a "beast" to do your dark deeds or use a loyal person who becomes a beast.

Becoming the Beast

One common factor with many military personnel who have seen total war and bloodshed is their inability to work their way back into society. They struggle with normal life after the highs, lows and pressure of combat but it is here where the true skill of the shinobi is found. A shinobi must endure a world that is darker than others and yet control it, focusing it and not allowing it to spill over into their cover while inside normal life. To truly perform as a shinobi is actually a task I think all but few can do. It falls to people with no natural morals and a total lack of empathy, or to those who have such an iron grasp on their emotions that they can perform in this capacity without letting evil memories leak into their social life. A shinobi is a person who hides in cold dank places while snow storms rage, they steal from those in need, swim rivers and climb out over ice, slay the innocent, lie to have people killed, throw poison gas into houses, wrangle venomous snakes, live with false identities, burn down entire villages, kill many people, have their own troops killed to gain an advantage, surrender young girls and boys to pedophiles, trek over vast mountain ranges, marry a woman and have children with her just to create a cover story, hide among enemy troops for days on end, bribe men of the cloth, creep into the houses of dangerous men and torture others. The question truly is, *are these the skills that you can possess and perform?*

Terrorism and Paramilitary

In essence, a shinobi is a both a terrorist and a paramilitary force. In enemy territory they perform acts of terrorism, yet in their own domains they are often formed into external units that function outside of normal army routine and may even be hired externally, such as the famous Iga and Koka groups. Therefore our definitions of terrorism and paramilitary do not quite cover their position. To all people, enemy strikes are an act of terror and to all military forces, people not from their regiment are outsiders. The shinobi has a hand in all of them, they perform acts of terror in other provinces, they spy in enemy lands, they form up as a separate unit while on campaign, they are specialized outsiders or even sometimes local bandit-thieves brought together for a campaign to fulfill a role. On the other hand, we find the dedicated internal shinobi, one who is loyal to the lord and who works in secret to make sure the affairs of the lord are kept well.

The Reality of Being Behind Enemy Lines

There are no words to describe how uncertain you feel in walking along an unfamiliar mountain path or in a forest.

True Path of the Ninja (1681)

The further a trooper ventures behind enemy lines, the more pressure is applied. It is different when the whole force is behind enemy lines and the full machine of military might supports each person. It is different for the single operator, security team and shinobi. They are either individuals who are totally covert in enemy lands, alone and following the most arduous route to avoid the enemy, or they are a small team with only each other as support. There is no back up, no air strikes, no Hollywood extractions from helicopters in wait, there is just their own guile, training and endurance.

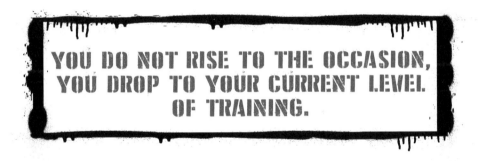

YOU DO NOT RISE TO THE OCCASION, YOU DROP TO YOUR CURRENT LEVEL OF TRAINING.

Cutting Throats

Cutting throats has a long history of being performed on defeated people, both upon captives as well as on field combatants. Images of prisoners having their throats cut are plentiful online and this often moves on to full decapitation. The following throat-cutting skill comes from a 1600s manual on samurai warfare (published in English as *Samurai War Stories*).

First, remember this act was applied to a defeated combatant or someone who was spiritually and mentally broken—a prisoner. They were forced to face downwards with their right arm held up behind their back. The right knee held their arm in position. Their head was pulled back by holding onto the nose and the area just above the mouth (or helmet peak if they were in samurai armor). Then the dagger was inserted—blade outwards—behind the windpipe, after which it was forcefully cut outwards. The head was held back until they died.

Decapitation

Decapitation has historically been a common terror tactic. The samurai would use a dagger to decapitate people. This was done by using a sawing motion to take the head off, getting through all the gristle, bone and muscle. The image of a noble samurai sitting defeated, waiting to be decapitated on the battlefield may be have been true, but it was not common. Often, the task involved a few people pinning down a single enemy and then sawing through the neck with a dagger. Some schools teach giving a *coupe de grace* if the enemy is higher ranking, so that they do not have to go through the ordeal of having their head taken off while they are alive. A *coupe de grace* is a mercy killing and can be performed by stabbing the heart or slicing the throat or femoral artery of a defeated enemy. (There are various theories that the latter of these three is actually either the ankle or the sole of the foot. This is still contested in samurai research but for practicality the femoral artery is given here).

PRIMARY EVIDENCE

According to an old samurai story, a samurai whose name was Mukai Noto-no-ka-mi said:

To hold and decapitate an enemy, pin him down by sitting astride him, keeping his dominant arm firmly under your right foot, turn up his helmet neck plates and then stab and cut the throat first, and then hold your wakizashi short-sword with a reverse grip, move the head into place by holding the helmet peak and cut off the head.

—*Samurai War Stories* (17th century)

Lording Over the Dead

It is one thing to defeat an enemy, but it is better psychological warfare to perform misdeeds upon the dead, to occupy their space, to take their women and to drink their wine. Historically, this sent a firm message to others and instilled fear in the rest of the enemy. Therefore, there was a focus on defiling corpses, raiding and using enemy stores—the terrorization of civilians that were under the protection of the enemy but are now at your mercy (this can also be reversed by being extremely kind to them if they were an oppressed people). Samurai of old would gather to perform celebration ceremonies, lording over the decapitated heads of the enemy. After this the heads were gibbeted for all to see. Only the bravest warriors or the highest-ranking leaders had their head sent back to their families.

In addition, piles of corpses and pyramids of heads were constructed, houses burned down, stores taken or destroyed, wells poisoned and the earth left barren making those in that area flee the terror and report it to the others. This spread fear and panic.

The following are the 12 reasons for samurai head celebrations according to Issui-Sensei:

PRIMARY EVIDENCE

The twelve principles for a head inspection:
1. *To celebrate a victory in battle.*
2. *To collect scattered soldiers together.*
3. *Not to become lost in triumph and too promote care.*
4. *To bring people back together so as to settle them down and follow the prescribed laws.*
5. *To praise an achievement as there is no other way to approve them.*
6. *For the lord-commander to show and acknowledge their soldiers.*
7. *To enhance the dignity of the lord-commander in the eyes of the soldiers.*

8. *To stimulate the discipline of soldiers by displaying fresh blood.*

9. *To investigate and gain details of military achievements.*

10. *To listen to the talk of the soldiers.*

11. *To encourage those soldiers who are idle.*

12. *To attack the enemy if they return.*

—*The Book of Samurai* series (17th century)

Applying Torture

When thinking of torture, people often consider it from the angle of being tortured; however, for the shinobi, the fact was they had to consider both being tortured and torturing others. There are scant records of the types of torture used by shinobi but we do know that fire and water are mentioned and their use is implied. Historical Japanese torture, on the other hand, has many aspects, including crushing, whipping, stretching, etc. Torture is extremely horrific, and can range from simple stress positions all the way up to rape, cannibalism, anal feeding and dismemberment. Therefore, it must be remembered that in ancient days, such acts would have been carried out by many people and the shinobi were among them. However, to what degree we do not have documentation. Today, the topic of torture of terrorists is a reality and hotly debated. You should not consider torture as merely a reality of the old world. Take from this that the shinobi and the modern agent have to consider torture of various levels. It takes a very specific kind of person to do this.

Assassination

When talking about assassination, it is best to separate the idea of assassination relayed in films from reality. Assassination is the murder of a political figure or of an individual without a personal grudge held against them. There is a fine line

WHAT'S THE DIFFERENCE?

MURDER: TO INTENTIONALLY AND MALICIOUSLY KILL ANOTHER PERSON

ASSASSINATION: TO KILL A NAMED FIGURE FOR POLITICAL OR FINANCIAL GAIN

REVENGE: TO KILL IN REPRISAL FOR A SLIGHT DONE TO AN INDIVIDUAL

EXECUTION: TO KILL A SUBJECT THROUGH AUTHORITY GIVEN BY A RULING CLASS

separating murder, revenge and assassination and often the three can stray into each other.

What is an assassin?

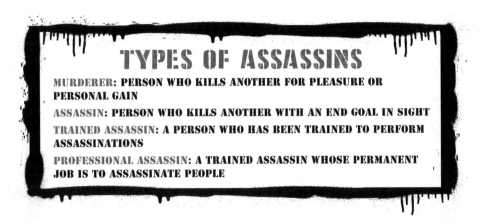

TYPES OF ASSASSINS

MURDERER: PERSON WHO KILLS ANOTHER FOR PLEASURE OR PERSONAL GAIN

ASSASSIN: PERSON WHO KILLS ANOTHER WITH AN END GOAL IN SIGHT

TRAINED ASSASSIN: A PERSON WHO HAS BEEN TRAINED TO PERFORM ASSASSINATIONS

PROFESSIONAL ASSASSIN: A TRAINED ASSASSIN WHOSE PERMANENT JOB IS TO ASSASSINATE PEOPLE

An assassin is someone who carries out the killing of another at the behest of someone else or for a politically motivated goal. Otherwise it is revenge killing or murder. An assassin can be a one-time assassin with no training or skills and may simply agree to kill a target. However, a trained person may be a full-time assassin or a skilled person who at times becomes involved in assassinations. Suicide bombers and terrorists are not considered to be assassins when they target general populations. They do have a political aim, yet their targets are random and public. Their aim is to bring about fear and not to change a political standpoint by the killing of a single person who holds an office. However, the same people become assassins when the target changes to a single political figure. There is a wide gap between a trained assassin, an *ad hoc* assassin, a murderer, a terrorist and a revenge killer.

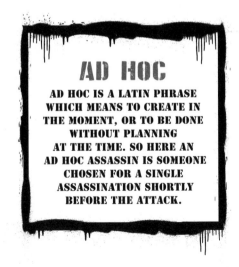

AD HOC

AD HOC IS A LATIN PHRASE WHICH MEANS TO CREATE IN THE MOMENT, OR TO BE DONE WITHOUT PLANNING AT THE TIME. SO HERE AN AD HOC ASSASSIN IS SOMEONE CHOSEN FOR A SINGLE ASSASSINATION SHORTLY BEFORE THE ATTACK.

Are the ninja assassins?

This is an often overlooked question to which the answer is both yes and no. The shinobi did indeed perform assassinations, and they did so training in infiltration and attack. However, their full time role is *not* an assassin, their full time role is as a commando, a spy or intelligence officer and on occasion they are used as assassins. Therefore, most, if not all shinobi were not full time assassins who were brought up being trained for the single purpose of killing. They were in fact trained spies and commando agents who dealt the vast sub-branches of the espionage world. That being said, there is the possibility that some shinobi devoted some of their time to this art and of course there is evidence to show that they did indeed perform assassinations from time to time.

PRIMARY EVIDENCE

It is possible to kill the enemy general with shinobi no jutsu and if done the benefit will be immeasurable. There is a secret in shinobi no jutsu on the skills required to kill the enemy's commander. In a case where your ninja can kill the enemy general, then it will bring an enormous benefit as the enemy will submit without fighting.

—The Book of Ninja (1676)

There are [two kinds of] spies, those of importance and those of lesser importance. They sometimes disturb enemy politics and twist the enemy so that their military plans are confused and wrong, also they move around spreading rumors and perform assassinations.

—Iga and Koka Ninja Skills (17th century)

A shinobi is normally presented to the lord in person, and has the opportunity to talk in close proximity, as the saying goes, "directly from the mouth to the ear." It is expected that at such a time the shinobi will not be allowed to wear a sword. However, he may hide a stabbing blade in his clothes or he may snatch the sword that the lord is wearing on his waist, with the intent to kill him. Therefore, you should never let your guard down and always remain vigilant.

—Iga and Koka Ninja Skills (17th century)

Their job is to travel discreetly to other provinces and gather information on the enemy's situation, sometimes they serve or follow the enemy tentatively to find gaps, they infiltrate enemy castles and set fires and they assassin people, etc.

—Unpublished manual

Assassinations

Assassinations are not uncommon in the world, from low level gang related murder of an enemy gang member, to organized crime kills, all the way up to political assassination. Assassins can be relatively low skilled but can also be highly-trained professionals who make quite a lucrative business from killing. There are basic areas that are covered by assassins to achieve a successful kill. You should be aware of these.

ASSASSINATION
PATIENCE
OBSERVATION
ROUTINE
OPPORTUNITY
KILL
ESCAPE

Observation—Observation is fundamental and key and assassination is 99% observation. Routine and a window of opportunity are focal points. A target will follow a routine, each week performing regular tasks, the agent's job is to find a place in that schedule to make a kill. It will be a time when the target is open, not defended, at their most vulnerable, and the situation makes for an easier exit. A target who knows they are a target will change routine constantly, alter travel routes, secure their compound and place measures to prevent the attempt on their life.

Bodyguards—If the target has bodyguards then these also have to be killed—unless using a long-eye sniper—but in the case where the kill is in close, a team will move in, most team members will move on to their bodyguard target but the lead member of the team will make the target kill.

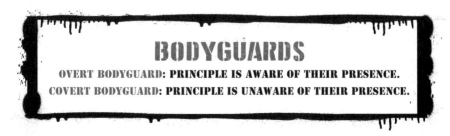

BODYGUARDS
OVERT BODYGUARD: PRINCIPLE IS AWARE OF THEIR PRESENCE.
COVERT BODYGUARD: PRINCIPLE IS UNAWARE OF THEIR PRESENCE.

Long-eye—The long-eye (sniper) is there for cover. If the routine suggests a place where a long eye can be used, this member of the team will help support the up close members by killing threats. Often a long-eye will act as cover because confirmation needs to be made on the kill.

The kill and confirmation—The kill is best made with the primary weapon, a side arm as back up and a dagger for emergencies. Confirmation is often required, this takes multiple forms, from blood samples to decapitated heads—of course these are not needed if the target is a popular figure but that is a rare event.

This need for confirmation hit the news in 2010 when a Gurkha solider removed the head of a high profile Taliban target and brought it back to base. *The Times* reported:

THE TIMES

Gurkha sent home after hacking off Taliban commander's head

A Gurkha soldier has been sent back from Afghanistan to his barracks in Britain after beheading a dead Taliban commander with his ceremonial knife to prove the man's identity. The private, from 1st Battalion, The Royal Gurkha Rifles, was flown back and suspended following the incident in the Babaji area of central Helmand this month. The Gurkhas had been told they were hunting a "high-value target" and had to prove they had killed the right man.

Low footprint—A kill team needs a low footprint. This is any information that leads back to the team—if there are leads from "safe houses," contacts, aides or any paperwork then the team is at risk. It is the case that sometimes the kill team will meet with local nationals or insertion team teams on the way in but will then murder the contact team that helped them enter when the assassination has been finished and they are on their way out. The contacts are of course unaware of this and during casual conversation, a kill team member will execute them to make sure the team cannot be identified.

Above all, the way of the shinobi is a step onto the horrific path and into a dark place. This will have great psychological effects on a person unless the person is on the spectrum and registers no emotion or has zero empathy. A lesser version of this is the world of intelligence, were oppressive tension and the fear of detection strain the nerves of even the calmest agents.

上忍

jōnin

中忍

chunin

下忍

genin

The Book of Ninja (1676) says
that shinobi are divided into
three levels: high-level, middle-
level and low-level agents.

CHAPTER 5

INTELLIGENCE

O ne major aspect of the shinobi is intelligence, including intelligence networks and intelligence gathering, alongside counter-intelligence. Many people often wrongly view the shinobi as only the commando style infiltrator, working in the depths of night; however, and most likely, their main focus is on intelligence. Both James Bond and the archetypal ninja hold a special place in the public eye because they have a specific identity and are perfect at both spying and commando missions. In the world of the shinobi, this perfect warrior is known as *jo-nin*—meaning "shinobi of extremely high ability" and many of their attributes are centered on intelligence and skills that allow them to work well in society as an agent. The following sections will briefly overview the world of the spy and investigator.

Universal Spycraft

One small consideration to be made is the understanding that because spies existed in many periods of history and all over the world, there is a general collection of skills that are shared by all spies in all ages, even though they had no contact with each other. For example the art of disguise, of passing on hidden information and code-breaking happen in many places because it is a universal need for working as a spy. This I will simply term as spycraft—the skills that unify all spies.

The Areas of Intelligence

The first step is to understand the basic layout of how intelligence systems work and how they function and for both the modern and the ancient world.

Headquarters

Spying is not done by a single person, all military forces will use many spies and they will need a headquarters (HQ) to send their information back to. The task of HQ is to direct all the spies like a symphony—they are the elements that steer the course of all the spies under their command. They are the hub of the spy network.

The spy network

The spy network is like a spider's web that covers the whole territory of interest to a military force. It extends to wherever the command center wishes it to go and it

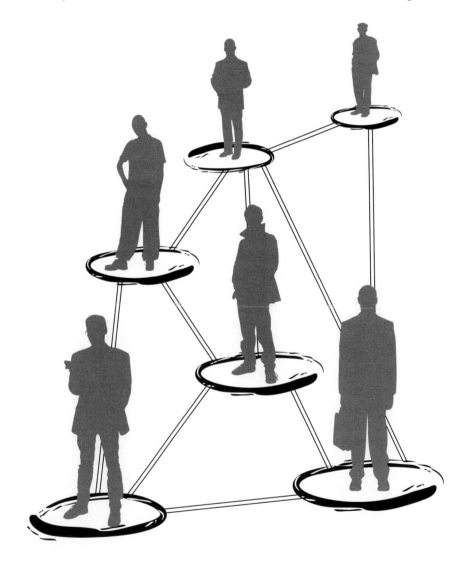

crosses over with other spy networks that often collaborate and share information. Imagine a mother spider at the center of her web. She represents HQ and all of the babies spiders spread out across the threads, they are the agents, the handlers and the low-level informants. Each web crosses over with another web coming into contact with enemy spy networks. Together they all interact, giving and hiding information, disguising their own movement and creeping on to each other's territory, yet each enemy "spider" is waiting for the strands of the web to vibrate, all of them listening, gathering information and bringing it back to the mother spider at HQ. It is here at HQ that a comprehensive picture of enemy tactics is assembled and presented to the main military commander and where the HQ team will identify fake information and double agents.

The spy-master

At the top of the spy network is the spy master, either an individual or command group. The spy master directs operations and make decisions on most cases. They will create a team below them to handle all the reports coming into HQ and will be presented with the most up-to-date picture of enemy movements. These spy-masters make the calls and run the service but they do have to do the bidding of the main military leader. In old Japan this was the lord they worked for and this task would have fallen to someone in the command group close to the lord who would in turn talk to the shinobi captains.

A symphony of spies

The network of spies would be conducted like a symphony—they would all work independently but their information is used in unison. It is only when the information comes in and is processed that the whole picture comes into play. It is useless to have a network of spies if the pulsing information and the direction of the spies is not conducted correctly. This is where the teaching of the ancient Chinese general Sun Tzu and his five types of spies come into play but it is also a teaching that is still used in modern times.

PRIMARY EVIDENCE

"You will be a cog in a very large machine, whose smooth functioning depends on each separate cog carrying out its parts effectively."
—*Special Operations Executive Lecture A.1, 1943*

Unless someone has the wisdom of the sage he cannot use spies; unless he is benevolent and righteous, he cannot employ spies; unless he is subtle and insight-ful, he cannot perceive the substance of intelligence reports. The subtleties of subtle! There are no areas in which one does not use spies."

—Sun Tzu, *The Art of War*

Identifying double agents

Double agents, traitors and spies who only guess at a situation instead of actually spying, are a problem for HQ. When all of the information is returned to the hub, analysts put it all together and start to "read between the lines." After this analysis has been completed, double agents, traitors and lazy spies will be highlighted. If there information does not fit into the general picture or seems "fishy" then it will stand out at this stage. Of course, a good double agent knows this and therefore tells the truth until a vital time when a lie is required. Telling the truth is actually a skill set that shinobi would focus on—the agent would try their best to be truthful at all times, until they approached the correct moment to do the most damage.

Safe houses

The first thing to know about safe houses is that they are not always safe. A safe house in enemy territory is simply a screen to hide operations or a place to stay out of sight. Safe houses do leave a paper trail and attract attention from locals. Therefore, never consider safe-houses to be safe, and do not stay too long in one. Any movement creates "vibrations" in the spy network so the more a safe house is used, the less safe it becomes. On home soil this is easier. Using a planted spy in enemy territory is a better idea; they establish themselves within the local commu-nity and become known. They are set up as merchants, traders, etc., and they will have at times visitors stay with them. This is better than a house that is randomly visited by a string of strangers. In old Japan safe houses were positioned all over the country and many warlords sent out their spies to insert themselves in enemy lands. The infamous spies used by the Edo Period shoguns of Japan called *oniwa-ban* were stationed at Edo Castle (Tokyo) but they had safe houses and merchants working in the major cities of Osaka and Kyoto. They also used Japan's messenger running service to hide the movement of their spies.

Finding double agents

When all the information brought back by spies in collated and compared, it will show where the double agents are and who or who is not performing their task correctly. In medieval Japan, manuals often mention shinobi who did not actually spy, but who went out on missions and simply guessed at enemy tactics from what seemed logical. This means that when an overall commander and a spy master are compiling information, sections will naturally highlight themselves where a spy's information does not fit in with the whole picture. It is then the task to identify if the spy is lazy, a double agent or being fed false information or, that they are the only ones who are correct while the others are being manipulated. Thus, the more spies a leader has, the less chance of dubious information being a problem and the easier it will be to detect where the problem lies. This is why Sun Tzu warns that by refusing to pay for a good number of spies it can cost a nation their entire resources.

The Five Types of Spies

Sun Tzu, the famous military tactician of ancient China, identified the five types of spies 2,000 years ago. To this day his categorization still not only stands true but is held as the standard. These five types of spies, when utilized by a military leader, are used in unison to bring about a better position of understanding for a military force. For a more detailed understanding of Sun Tzu's chapter on spies see my work *Iga and Koka Ninja Skills*.

PRIMARY EVIDENCE

Raising a host of a hundred thousand men and marching them great distances entails heavy loss on the people and a drain on the resources of the State. The daily expenditure will amount to a thousand ounces of silver. There will be commotion at home and abroad, and men will drop down exhausted on the highways. As many as seven hundred thousand families will be impeded in their labor. Hostile armies may face each other for years, striving for the victory which is decided in a single day. This being so, to remain in ignorance of the enemy's condition simply because one grudges the outlay of a hundred ounces of silver in honors and emoluments, is the height of inhumanity.
—Sun Tzu, *The Art of War* (Translation by the Chinese Text Project)

THE 13TH CHAPTER

Sun Tzu's use of spies is found in the 13th and final chapter of *The Art of War*. In Japanese it is called *Yokan*.

Local spies

These are non-military people, local inhabitants of a target area. Approach these people and either offer them a bribe as a one-off payment for information or build a continuous relationship with them, supplying them with cash and goods in exchange for a constant update of their area and any movements made by the enemy, or anything of note. Have living spies contact local spies in large numbers, build a network of these local spies so that permanent spies can do circuits of the enemy territory and pick up vast amounts of information on their "rounds." This is fed back to HQ.

INKO NO KAN
LOCAL SPIES

However, take note that this is considered as "outside information" and also covers those agents who have been planted in that area.

Internal spies

These are people who are already inside the enemy force, such as the military or those who work for the government or directly for the target. They are privy to internal information that is normally kept secret to the outside world. However these types of spies are close to danger at all times and normally require larger amounts of money and an escape and asylum plan. This is considered as inside information as they are privy to all the internal goings on, depending on how high ranking they are. The more of these or the higher ranking the better.

NAIRYO NO KAN
INTERNAL SPIES

Converted spies

These are enemy spies sent to observe you—they work for the enemy and their role is to spy against you. First you have to identify these spies as they will be living in your community or visiting. They will be interacting with locals or even people in your own forces who are betraying you. They may be infiltrating at night and overhearing conversations or they will be in full view of the public with hidden intentions. When they have been identified, approach them in a friendly manner and offer them rewards of

HANTOKU NO KAN
CONVERTED SPIES

many types, from wine, women and song, to money or achievement in personal and political aims, then *convert* them to your side. This now starts a dialogue that becomes a game of who is telling the truth and your task is to convert them—their task is to stay loyal. Therefore, you have to discover their weakness, be it an idealistic nature all the way down to base sex and cash. Once you are in a relationship with a converted spy they can give you much of the information you require and they are considered by some ancient commentators as the most important spies of all. They will tell you passwords, map out compound internals, inform you of the enemy's next move and importantly, let you know which of the enemies close retainers can be bribed and who will be susceptible to being used as an internal spy. Consider converted spies as the gateway to the enemy.

Doomed spies

A doomed spy is a spy used to feed false information back to the enemy. They can be one of your own spies, a captured enemy spy or even just a non-combatant who is used to transfer false information— they are not expected to return. Doomed spies are sent at vital points in a war, in a situation where the enemy may need to work under the pressure of time and act on the information they have just received. This can also be done by sending information the enemy expects to hear. By using internal spies you can discover what the enemy is thinking and you

SHICHO NO KAN
DOOMED SPIES

can add to their expectations via the doomed spy who is given false information. Finally, this can be a loyal agent who knows that they are going to die but are willing to perform that task for honor and country, such as assassinations. In World War II these were known as Bonzos and were POWs from Germany who had gone through rigorous interviewing sessions, who had been selected and trained

CONTROLLING
A DOOMED SPY
FEED THEM FALSE INFORMATION
HIGH REWARD
HOSTAGES

as agents and then sent back to Germany to blend in with the locals and to carry out instructions, cause mayhem and to engage in propaganda. The real key to the doomed spy is the choice to give the agent real or false information.

Living spies

Living spies are fully-trained agents. They are professional spies who perform the task as their main job. They are well trained and can work in their chosen field, such as an undercover agent, a commando or a linguist—they travel to enemy territory and return. They know all that is needed to be known about their art and they fulfill the military leaders needs by using the tools and skills of their trade. They are then ranked into the three sections of *jo-nin, chu-nin* and *ge-nin* (the three ranks of shinobi). The best of them perform at top levels. Living spies are often highly trusted and the best have direct contact with the military leader and/or the spy-master. At the lower end the shinobi who perform as living agents do their duty to the best of their personal ability. Most people think of the ninja as living spies, the full-time professional spy like James Bond.

TENSEI NO KAN
LIVING SPIES

Surveillance

The following section is an overview of spying in what is mainly known as *yo-nin*—infiltration in plain sight. This means that the enemy can physically see you but you are ignored as a general member of the public, blending into the background and becoming the "gray man." While you keep out of sight, you are generally not hiding in stealth; however, that is an option. When carrying out surveillance you have the following choices:

- Spy as nobody
- Spy as somebody
- Infiltrate long term
- Infiltrate short term
- Be static
- Be on the move

It will depend on the goal of the project as to which one you take; however, the one of least risk is to be a "nobody" on the move, constantly meeting new people.

This however does not gain internal information, but brings a larger picture with a broader scope.

Mixing between stealth and plain sight

While infiltration normally consists of being in plain sight, there are a few times where you may have to move to stealth. Shinobi of old used to change between *in-nin* and *yo-nin*, meaning that they may enter a castle through the front gate under a pretext. They would then find a dark place in the camp, climb walls and move through the next layer of security and then come back into plain sight once they had overheard the passwords. This is changing between both plain sight and stealth and is done in the same mission and possibly multiple times.

Catching important information

Hattori-sensei of Iga decent gives a good visual image of what it is like to be a shinobi performing constant surveillance. He likens it to watching a still pond and that once in a while a fish will break the surface, creating ripples. The pond in this analogy is society, the humdrum of everyday life, the fish is a piece of information that is out of context or which provides the shinobi with an insight into enemy plans. The idea can be pushed further by imagining that there are teams of shinobi all watching the pond from different angles and each time a "fish" breaks the water they record the event and form a better picture of the movements below the water. This lesson can be used in both observation of the enemy and in conversation. Searching through trash, listening to conversations in public, "wire taps" on private lines, collection of public and private data, etc.—all of these things are observation, and when useful informative is found, it is like the fish breaking the surface of the water, letting you see into the presence of the enemy.

Local clothes & customs

Shinobi agents had specialists who focused on understanding the various fashions of each area, their local customs, places of significance and the dialects they spoke. This is often an underappreciated skill by the modern community, but people who actually work in the field know the true value of not standing out in an environment. From not using certain soaps and shampoos in jungles to tying scarves and ties in the correct way, remember, slight but obvious mistakes will lead to instant identification. During World War II, the Allied forces used POWs who had manufactured personal items such as clothing and accessories in their civilian lives to create similar goods for the war effort. These items were then used by Allied agents in occupied territories so that they did not stand out.

PRIMARY EVIDENCE

The most important thing you should keep in mind when you go on a shinobi mission is to know the language of the target province well and the ways of the local people. This includes their appearances, the way of wearing clothes, the way of shaving the head, the way of making up their hair, the way of making up a sword or short sword and the way of refinement and luxury, all of these elements change from location to location.

—*Secret Traditions of the Shinobi* (16th and 17th century)

Areas of interest

When spying in enemy territory it is best to approach areas of special interest—tourist and pilgrim spots, cross roads, markets, religious centers—as these places are where strangers openly meet and talk, exchanging information about current events. For this reason spies, focus on such places so that their probing is not identified. An ancient master named Kiichi Hogen said there were five areas which capture the minds of other people. To this day all of them are used in the world of advertising:

1. *Beautiful men and women*
2. *Luxury palaces and mansions*
3. *Beautiful and quiet scenery consisting of rocks and water*
4. *Music and dance*
5. *The fine arts*

—*True Path of the Ninja* (1681)

Hidden objects

Spies have to smuggle various items into the area they are infiltrating and openly carry them. Normal-looking objects such as porcelain ornaments are shaped
around the item the spy needs, and when the agent has taken the item past the
area of inspection, the casing can be smashed and the inside item used. This also
includes items made to look exactly like items such as tins of food, oil, etc., things
that should not just be opened at an inspection. Shinobi used to hide letters and
information in religious statues, in the guts of fish and sewn into their underwear,
etc.. Samurai messengers used to hide letters in the hole at the top of their helmets
or stitched into the rope ties of their hats. Hidden objects fit into objects that are
considered normal.

Performing a drop

The section on *hidden objects* outlines items or equipment spies carry themselves
while a *drop* uses items or equipment dropped off for spies to later collect. This
can be in urban areas or in the wilderness.

Codes and code breaking

Cryptography is the science of hiding the meaning of messages from the eyes of
others and covers a wide range of subjects. Today cryptography is much more
advanced than it was in the past, and technology plays a major role in encryp-
tion. Various types of codes include: *transposition* (shifting the letters around in a
message), *rail fence cypher* (the letters of a code are moved on to different lines),
columnar transposition (the letters form a block and are then typed out the different ways), *Myszkowski transposition* (a columnar form with numbers added) and,
substitution cyphers (letters are substituted in multiple ways where more frequently
used letters have multiple substitutions). Code breaking is a colossal subject performed by highly-trained specialists. From an agent's point of view, code breaking
is not as important as they would possess the secret key to understanding a code.
It is not their task to break codes themselves—it is they who are sending the coded
messages themselves.

Overt and covert observation in the field

Moving into enemy territory can be performed covertly or overtly. As previously
stated, in ancient Japan this was known as *in-nin* (dark shinobi work) and *yo-nin*
(light shinobi work), the former being unseen and unobserved by the enemy (dark)
and the latter being seen but unnoticed by the enemy (light). Being *dark* means

that you are hiding, out of sight and travelling without the enemy's knowledge; being *light* means that you are in disguise or are blending in with the population to be unnoticed by the enemy. There are various ways to describe this today, such as "nonparticipation observation" and "participation observation" but it all means hiding from a single target or larger enemy by either being in plain sight of a single target or out of sight of an enemy.

Overt and covert observation with a mark

Being employed and assigned to a person can be done overtly or covertly. Bodyguarding or shadowing with the mark's knowledge means that you are there to protect them and observe their surroundings, making sure they are safe or that they are free to leave you with the task of controlling the environment around them. However, covert observation is when the mark has no idea that you are there or observing them, such as the targets of private investigators, fraud investigators or covert bodyguards, as with parents who wish a high-risk child to be watched over without them knowing.

Emotional detachment

Working in both overt and covert observation means that you will be in close proximity to a mark or client and you will live and breathe their life. This could go on for an extended period of time and, depending on your personality, you may

become emotionally attached to the client or mark. If the task finishes—such as a parent who no longer wishes you to track their daughter—you may be left feeling an emotional attachment to her and her safety, hoping that no harm will come to her after she has left your "protection." However, emotional detachment is required to walk away and treat as a job and remain impersonal is essential.

Skip tracing

A skip tracer is a person searching for someone who has "skipped town," which means to leave without notice and or to disappear. Skip tracing is the task of finding them and is also the skills of using legal and publicly available means to track a person down. That means using public records of all kinds, such as, household bills, club memberships, registers, social media, friends, colleagues, contacts and all "non-invasive" methods of collecting data to build a picture of a mark. When collated, this data will form into a detailed account of the structure of a person's life. From spending habits, social life style and frequented places etc., this allows a person tracing the mark to narrow down the places they may be or, to form an idea of what has happened to a person. A great amount of effort is needed in such a project to assess the information and build a picture. Think of this as doing a jigsaw, a vast amount of time is used to make small pieces into a larger image.

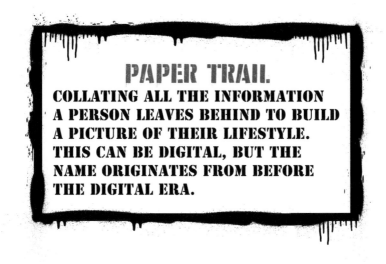

PAPER TRAIL.
COLLATING ALL THE INFORMATION A PERSON LEAVES BEHIND TO BUILD A PICTURE OF THEIR LIFESTYLE. THIS CAN BE DIGITAL, BUT THE NAME ORIGINATES FROM BEFORE THE DIGITAL ERA.

Pretext

A pretext is your false identity, the "life" behind any disguise you have. It means the pretext in which you approach a mark. This is art of crafting a whole identity and a narrative to the person you are pretending to be. This is a complex thing to do and requires a high level of skill if the fake identity is not to be seen through.

WARNING
ONCE YOU CONTACT THE MARK, YOU CANNOT CHANGE YOUR PRETEXT AND YOU HAVE TO MAINTAIN THAT FALSE IDENTITY EVERY TIME YOU COME INTO CONTACT WITH ANYONE CONNECTED TO THE JOB.

In ancient Japan, generals sometimes used *yamabushi*, mountain pilgrims, as spies—they did this because *yamabushi* are expected to travel the lands and their movement is not suspicious. While it was possible to train someone to look and sound like a *yamabushi*, upon investigation it can be too difficult to maintain the fake identity of such a specialization as mountain monks. Instead they would recruit actual *yamabushi* monks as spies because they already had the training in their religious ways and were used to long distance travel.

PRIMARY EVIDENCE

山伏之事
Yamabushi no koto
Yamabushi mountain hermits
The number of these is not definite.

They perform services to the gods during a campaign, they also perform incantations for those samurai who would like prayer service. Sometimes [real yamabushi*] are used as kanja—spies because fake* yamabushi *can be easily detected, thus, if there are any who are willing, use these* yamabushi *[as spies].*
                              —*The Book of Samurai* series (17th century)

It is extremely difficult to maintain a fake identity; once you have presented your-self in a role you cannot use any other until you have finished the job. Also, even then, the mark will become suspicious if you constantly keep popping up, even if the pretext holds firm. Therefore, forming a pretext is serious and should not be done lightly.

Observation point

The observation point (OP) is a position where you can view a target or target area. In urban environments this could be from a building, a rooftop or in the open such as in a café or from a bench. In the wilderness these should be waterproofed and camouflaged. Both can be covert or overt; they can be long-standing or temporary and must have a clear and constant view of the target. Multiple OPs are better but must always remain secret unless they are permanent watch positions. Be careful of giveaway signs such as lens reflection or overwatching the enemy if in plain sight. An OP must have an exit strategy; you must be able to get away from one quickly.

Mobile observation points

Mobile observation points are normally inside vehicles. Cars can be used to "tail" people and bicycles can be used to follow people on foot. However, "mobile" means it can be moved and that for lengths of time the vehicle may be stationary. One example of this is the car trunk (car boot for people in the UK). Small holes or viewing ports are carefully drilled into the trunk and an agent is placed in the

Vectors courtesy of Vecteezy.com.

trunk. The vehicle is then left in a parking spot that allows the viewing port to overlook the building or target area you wish to observe. As no one is sitting in the actual car seats it appears to be an empty parked car but inside, the agent is noting down routine and information on the target or any other details that help with the surveillance.

Disguises

A disguise is different from *local clothes and customs*—the latter is to dress as a local, the former is to disguise yourself as someone you are not. While the two do cross over they fall into different categories. The following points are things to be considered when in disguise:

- Body shape
- Hair style and hairline shape
- Atmosphere of the character
- Skin tone
- Costume/clothes
- Mannerisms

A disguise changes the shape/color/style of your face, hair and body, to change accent, to be a personality you are not. On the other hand, embracing local customs is to look like yourself, but wear the clothes of the target area and use their dialect and customs. Make sure to understand if you are to be in disguise or if you are to adopt local ways, both change your appearance but do so in different ways.

Camera

As cliché as it is, the camera is the best friend to the private investigator. Of course, flash photography has given way to digital technology , but an extensive knowledge of the various cameras available, both overt and covert is required—including their use. The correct cataloguing and storage and backup of images is also a necessity. Photos give you the details of a situation that memory cannot and nowadays digital photos are encoded with much needed information such as time and date.

Security cameras

The presence and location of, and access to, security cameras is a massive issue today. In the past, the shinobi had to deal with patrols, both light and dark, but they were still just people. Now the camera is ever watchful and technology ever progressing.

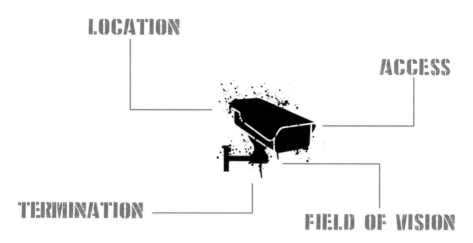

LOCATION

ACCESS

TERMINATION

FIELD OF VISION

Carry writing equipment

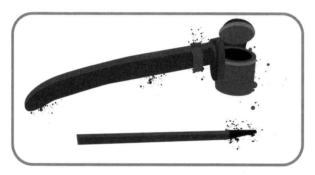

A *yatate* Japanese brush and ink holder carried by many
people but used by shinobi to record information.

One of the most obvious but underrated elements for an investigator is simply carrying a pen and notebook. Of the many tools of the trade, the simple pen and paper can be the most valuable. Shinobi manuals do mention the *yatate*—which is a small tool that holds a brush and an ink pot and like the shinobi of old, the investigator must have some way to record what they see, because small bits of information always make for a larger and clearer image. It must be remembered that when making notes, record in code.

PRIMARY EVIDENCE

The Japanese Sumi ink and brush are useful for every purpose. You should not go on a shinobi activity without a yatate *ink and brush.*
—Secret Traditions of the Shinobi (16th and 17th century)

Coded notes

When involved in surveillance, use coded notes; never refer to the mark by their name and never make any records understandable to anyone who may find them or take them from you. For example, take your code words from the weather or a sport such as football (or even something socially undesirable as trainspotting). Then refer to different elements of your surveillance using these words. Some examples are weather terms (wind, rain, sunshine, cloudy, etc.), sports terms (team names scores, stadiums, etc.), and railroad terms (train types, train numbers, station names, etc.). Such codes may be overlooked by some people but even if it does arouse suspicion in an unwanted reader, it is not so obvious to what term replies to which part of your operation.

PRIMARY EVIDENCE

A [letter] should be written with ground soybeans or with the liquid used to strain teeth or even with the juice of the Yuzu fruit. To read [such a letter] hold it over a fire or soak it in water. The liquid used to stain teeth cannot be seen unless it is soaked in water. I must state that to read the letters written with this tooth staining liquid you should coat the underside of the paper in ink, this is because the characters will not absorb the ink, making them clear to see.

—*Samurai and Ninja* (17th century)

Infiltrating a group

There is always the option of infiltrating the group that the target belongs to. However, once in the group then pretext has been set and there is no way to change it. This means less freedom; however, it does mean that an agent is on the inside. It is best not to directly introduce yourself to the target but to come in via another member. The target will trust you more if introduced to you by their own friend and they will automatically connect with you if you have a shared interest. Most groups are built on a shared interest, such as sports, clubs, business, occupation, etc. Issui-sensei teaches that a person's friendship group is almost always made up of work colleagues or people who share the same interest, so if that person loves football, be an ardent supporter of their team, if they love swordsmanship, become proficient in their style of swordsmanship. The point is that no matter what, if you share a deep love for a subject, you will share a bond with the target and when people have a shared bond and shared experiences. They build trust and trust leads to the revealing of secrets. Therefore, entering a group is always an option, and both spies and law enforcement agencies across the world have agents who infiltrate criminal and enemy organizations, from street gangs to crime warlords, all the way up to double agents in enemy spy rings. Infiltrating a group is multi-layered but fundamental to spy craft. However, remember once the pretext is set you are set in that role, your whole life has to be that role and you have to convince the mark that you know what you are talking about on the chosen subject.

Counter surveillance skills

When engaged in covert work you also have to check if you yourself are being followed, making sure that no one is tracking you while you are tracking others. The following selection are basic skills to check if people are following you or to minimize that risk

Use alternative routes—Never use the same route each day nor the same routine. Change the route you walk around the area; do not visit the same shops at the same times and do not form patterns that can be followed. Forming patterns makes you predictable.

Double back—Whether walking or in a vehicle, double back and go the long way around. Never take the shortest route, turn corners, go back on yourself and make sure that the same cars or people do not keep reappearing. This takes time and can be frustrating but is worth doing.

Change modes of transport—Change your mode of transport between vehicles and swap between systems of public transport.

Steal a bicycle—If you are being followed on foot or by car while walking in an urban area, steal or take a push-bike (bicycle). You will be faster than the enemy and you can go where cars cannot. Use this to escape, then ditch the bike (remember to wipe it down).

Leaving public transport and aircraft—When getting off a plane or public transport, stop and buy a drink, take a moment to "rest" as you walk to the exit and use this time to observe who is around you. Next, subtly use body language to imply you have forgotten or dropped something, turn around and walk back towards the gate where the plane is. When you get there, look to see if anyone has followed you. If someone has, "find" what you are looking for and mark them. If there is no one, turn around and make your way back to the exit, stopping at the toilet; observe if anyone that you previously identified is waiting for you along the corridor. It is best to remember features such as colors and articles of clothing. Natori-Ryu teaches that when you are on a scouting mission as a samurai, check the following so that you can remember the person with ease because you will not remember faces as well.

PRIMARY EVIDENCE

The five points which help you to remember people are:
1. *The appearance of their horse's hair.*
2. *Their armor.*
3. *The mark on their spear.*
4. *Their banner.*
5. *The crest on the front of their helmet.*

—The Book of Samurai series (17th century)

Door observation

Doors tend to open towards the person that controls them. For example, the main door to a house, a living space or bedroom opens inwards, because the person who resides there has control, they can block the inside and make a barrier so that an intruder cannot push their way in. Whereas a storeroom or closet will open outwards, this is because the person who controls it tends to reside on the outside of the closet space. This is not a set rule and individual choice or other elements have had an effect on the planning of a building; however it can be accepted as a general rule. This means two things: first, a quick walk down a corridor can give you an idea of the position of living spaces and closet spaces by the way the hinges are positioned. Second, if the external viewing of a building and the subsequent mental mapping of the floor layout do not match the expected door openings, then a hidden room may be present. Furthermore, if the door to something labeled "stores" opens inwards, it is possibly a fake—unless there is reason for it to

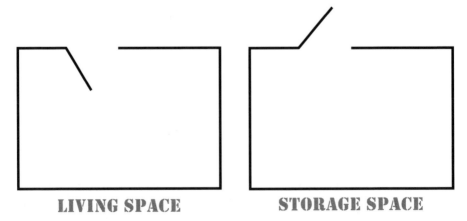

LIVING SPACE   **STORAGE SPACE**

have been made so. This skill is not an absolute, but it can answer some general questions about irregularities in a building.

The door and tape trick

This is a simple skill. Place clear tape at the top of a doorway as shown in the images below. In the first, the lower end of the tape is folded over to create a flap. When a door is opened the flap of tape will move to the inside of the door; when it is shut it will be between the door and the frame. This way you can identify if the door has been opened or not. The second shows how to do this on the side of the door.

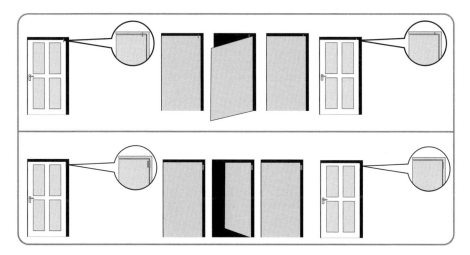

Light switches

If someone has infiltrated your house, observation point or safe house, they may plant spying equipment in mundane objects such as electrical extension cords. They may also place listening devices behind the light switches of the room, as this is a convenient hole in the wall that already has a cover. Therefore, to test if someone has infiltrated and has been inside the light switch, use the two ways illustrated here to defend yourself.

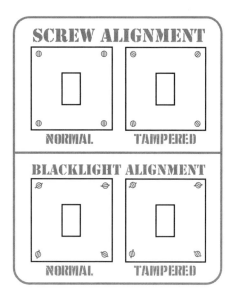

SCREW ALIGNMENT

NORMAL   TAMPERED

BLACKLIGHT ALIGNMENT

NORMAL   TAMPERED

Screw alignment—The first is *screw alignment*. Tighten all the screws so that they are aligned either vertical or horizontal or a mixture of both and then keep a record of them. If the screws have moved position, know that someone has tampered with them.

Black light alignment—The second is black light alignment. This is to have the screws at random positions but to draw a line over the screw to the back plate with a clear marker. This line shows up under black light—if the alignment has changed, it has been tampered with.

All of the above elements are the basics of surveillance and intelligence gathering. From the complex use of teams of spies to basic tricks that help keep you safe. The key to intelligence is a low profile, a sturdy defense or mobility and endurance to wait and gather. It is this element of endurance that brings us to the next section—the way of the mind.

CHAPTER 6

THE WAY OF THE MIND

U p to this point I have focused on physical skills or the idea of having to perform deeds that normal people would not. This chapter will focus on the mental aspects of espionage and the mindset of the infiltrator commando and spy.

The Mindset Required

It is harsh to say, but most people could not be a spy at a higher level. Almost any-one can be a spy at the lower levels, gathering public data or watching a certain area. Likewise, many people can succeed as military personnel working in a large group but few can push to the extremes of the commando and fewer still can be deep undercover agents or high-end infiltrators in extremely dangerous situations. In truth, those at the highest level are born with the mindset that is needed with the mental capacity to achieve this role. When picking candidates, physical skill and physical endurance is not a high priority as people can be made fit and healthy. They can be pushed if they have the right mental qualities. That is not to say people cannot acquire the mindset needed but it is a hard road to become mentally ready to be a high-end commando-spy.

The Path of Perseverance

The concept of mental perseverance and endurance is strongly connected to the shinobi; they are named for it. As shinobi has both the meaning of stealth and perseverance, and while shinobi started out having individual job names in an-cient Japan, they all gathered under the term *shinobi no mono* by the end of the 1500s. It is difficult to describe what is actually required to achieve a high level of perseverance, but during those moments of your life where you have broken down under pressure, where life has become too much and you are cracking, needing to talk to unburden an invisible but heavy load, take that feeling and add the pressure of a hostile environment and with killers trying to find you. It is here that a shinobi needed to display no outward sign of stress of any form and even at the point of breaking, they remained calm. That is why they are shinobi, because no matter how broken inside, their external appearance is tranquil. The following is a reduced quote from Issui-sensei in 1681:

PRIMARY EVIDENCE

Shinobi sometimes talk about a province they have never been to, tell a strange story about a place they do not know, pretend to be friends with a stranger, buy things with gold or silver they don't have, eat food nobody gives, get drunk and go on a drunken spree even without drinking alcohol and learn every kind of art in the world. Also, oddly without being asked they disguise themselves as a monk or priest, even if they are not used to doing it, they have nowhere they cannot go, they camouflage themselves as women, such as an old mountain hag, they go out acting covertly all night and sleep out in a field without shelter. Sometimes as a Ninja you may be startled at the call of a deer and search in panic for a hiding place whilst moaning in agony or grief, a sadness which no one is aware of. You will get annoyed with the moonlight and seek for the shelter of the shadows within a forest. Yet you have nobody to talk with or to unburden such toils and dismay, are any of these things a marvel for you at all? The people of the world around you may not know of your plight and engage you in conversation but you must answer them without revealing any stress, this is also one of deceptions of the shinobi.

—*True Path of the Ninja* (1681)

The ideogram for shinobi "stealth and perseverance" in the term "shinobi no jutsu" by Monk Yamamoto, Issui-sensei's grave keeper.

Substantial and Insubstantial

Deception is the point and the foundation of *shinobi no jutsu*. It is found in a concept called *kyojitsu*—when all is broken down to its bare points, a shinobi must do two things:

1. Discover where the enemy is presenting *deception* and what the *truth* actually is.
2. Present the enemy with deception and hide their truth.

From speech to troop movements, from disguise to commando raids, the entire world of warfare is found in understanding the difference between *kyo* and *jitsu*. A single operator will get close to the enemy to perform reconnaissance, they will observe the whole army; however, the observer must wonder if this is really a true representation of their military strength. Itinerant spies who have wandered the country will have already made reports on the financial well-being of the enemy; they will have investigated the population, the potential tax income and amount of military service of the area and when this data is compiled back at HQ. The command group will have a good understanding of the capability of the enemy strength. This information is passed on to the single operator whose task it is to observe the force that the enemy have put on the field of battle and if the force they have fielded does not match the results of the land survey then deception is "in the air." Once it has been established that not all troops are present on the field of battle, then it is the task of the shinobi to search out their position and report their whereabouts to the commander in the field. This is just one example of how deception has to be discovered and as stated above—it applies to all things.

A shinobi infiltrating a castle has to observe the defenses and discover if a gap that they find in the systems of defense is actually a real gap or is it a trick to lure them in. Just as a swordsman will lower their guard to bait an enemy, the enemy will bait a shinobi with apparent gaps—it is here that the best shinobi rise to the top. If an agent can spot the difference between what is real and what is presented as real they will win over the enemy and grow in fame within their own force. This difference between what is true and what is not true is known as *substantial* and *insubstantial*. It cannot be stressed enough that this lesson must be at the heart of all you do in the world of espionage and the shinobi masters of old made sure to pass on this teaching.

Emotions

Here the term "emotions" is the closest word to a concept laid down in old Japan, but it is not simply just emotion. The Japanese term "*jo*" means "a state of being," a state of emotion that is the makeup of your character. Religious thought in old

Japan held that there are 7 states that exist inside a human personality and that they float inside of a person, each one developing and growing as people gain experience, each one rising to the "surface" depending on the situation. They also believed that if all 7 emotions are controlled equally and they become "level" and calm like that of a smooth body of water, then a person will have come close to perfection. However, most people (if not all people) have one dominate state at their core, one emotion that they rest their personality on. This emotion or natural state is their true personality and while they do have the others, it is their "default setting." However, often, because this is the core of their being, they will hide this emotion and it only becomes prominent in emergency situations. A shinobi is looking for this core element. Paul Ekman, a leading figure in human behavior has reduced the emotions to 6 basic types, while other researchers have reduced this even more. However, here we shall focus on Ekman. The following table contains the various sets of states of emotion.

The Emotions—jo 情				
N°	English	Ideogram	Latinization	Connotations
The Six Basic Emotions of Paul Ekman				
1	Happiness	N/A	N/A	To feel happy in a situation.
2	Anger	N/A	N/A	To be angry at a situation.
3	Sadness	N/A	N/A	To feel sad and depressed.
4	Fear	N/A	N/A	To be afraid of something.
5	Disgust	N/A	N/A	To be disgusted by something.
6	Surprise	N/A	N/A	To be surprised by something .
The Seven Emotions				
1	Delight	喜	Ki/yorokobu	To feel happy in a situation.
2	Anger	怒	Do/Ikaru	To be angry at a situation.
3	Gloom	憂	Yu	To feel grief, anxiety, sadness.
4	Overthinking	思	Shi	To consider, to think, to worry.
5	Sorrow	悲	Hi	To feel sadness and sorrow.
6	Fear	恐	Kyo	To feel fear, scared, in danger.
7	Surprise	驚	Kyo	To be surprised, startled, shocked.

N°	English	Ideogram	Latinization	Connotations
				The Seven Emotions used in shinobi no Jutsu
1	Delight	喜	Ki/yorokobu	To feel happy in a situation.
2	Anger	怒	Do/Ikaru	To be angry at a situation.
3	Sorrow	哀	Kanashimu	To feel grief, distress, sadness, mournful.
4	Pleasure	楽	Tanoshimu	To feel enjoyment and find pleasure.
5	Love	愛	Ai	To love, care, embrace and affection.
6	Evil intent	悪	Nikumu	To be vindictive and vicious.
7	Greed	欲	Musaboru	To acquire, want etc.

Finding the Core Emotion

One of the agent's tasks is to take control of a target in the enemy ranks, using a converted spy to gain the information they need to discover who the best target to approach is. Once that target has been identified, they have to establish their emotions. This is done through observation and situation. Observation will allow you to see how they react in many situations, controlling a situation to add pressure will allow you to see their true nature. Of course, people will go through all emotions, but it is their foundational one the shinobi is interested in. If a person does not have anger at their core, then anger only flashes but will be gone soon. If greed is not at their core they may only lust for something for a short time then forget about it. A shinobi needs to know what they want, continuously and deep down. If a person's foundation is pleasure, bribe them with pleasure, if they have a natural inclination towards dark elements then that is what you bribe them with. If a person is naturally sorrowful, bribe them with your time and support, building a relationship. A person's core emotion is their weakness. Never bribe a person who is generous. Do not offer dark pleasure to a person of happiness, and do not offer beautiful and happy entertainment to a person of a darker nature. Taking into account social engineering and the protocols and ethics of society will allow you to know the inner heart of a target for you to manipulate them fully.

Observing Both Nature and Mind

- *With alcohol, allow someone to become drunk to observe their nature (性)*
- *With pleasure, please someone with pleasure to observe their mind (心)*
  —*The Book of Samurai* series (17th century)

There is a difference between a person's nature and their mind. A person's nature reveals their core characteristics while their mind reveals their intellect. Getting someone drunk can show their core nature, remembering that they hide it. Statements like "it was the drink talking" are not accurate. Instead this should be "it was the drink that made me say the truth." A person's mind is shaped by society. This is the nature-nurture argument. In old Japan they believed that a person had a core nature and that society then manipulated their mind to fit in and conform. Ethics change from country to country and from time to time. What is considered inappropriate today may have been perfectly normal in an earlier time. Therefore, to see what people actually want to do, offer them something pleasurable and if they are comfortable they will divulge their true thoughts. They can then be bribed in the correct way as you will have an understanding of their core and the advantage of knowing their learned likes.

Mental Aspects of Capture

The major concern for an agent is capture which can lead to torture and execution. Capture represents either prolonged imprisonment or a cruel, painful and premature end to life. It is "game over." The pressure of being captured is beyond description and this is where a person often breaks down.

The four reasons for capture

There are four main reasons for capture by hostiles:

1. Political.
2. Financial.
3. Power affirmation.
4. As a prisoner of war.

Political—No matter if it is religious or political, this form of capture is done to force a political agenda. This can branch off into many subdivisions, but at its core this is one faction trying to manipulate another faction through a captive. The larger issue for you as a captive is if it is a political statement or a hostage exchange. If it is a political statement then the chances are you will die a gruesome death, so just start killing and pray. If it is a hostage exchange your life has value.

Financial—This is the best type of capture for you, as it has the incentive is to keep you alive and ransom you back to your family or faction. If there is a high possibility that you will be ransomed maintain mental strength.

Power affirmation—Gangs, corrupt groups, thugs or the religiously insane may capture people to display dominance over other humans. This is often a bonding exercise for the group as extreme situations create bonds. If you are captured by this type of group their aim is to put you through "hell" while they laugh at you and congratulate themselves. In this situation you have almost no chance of survival if the group is serious, so again try to escape or at least "take some with you." An alternative version of this is the serial killer, quiet individuals who lure people into traps to take power over them.

Prisoners of war—Prisoners of war do not come under the above reasons because they are a by-product of a battle and the aim was never to capture them. The situation you will find yourself in as a prisoner of war will vastly differ depending on the war you are fighting. This could be anything from a few years in an officers mess, drinking cocktails all the way down to a hellish end with starvation and forced labor and gruesome extermination.

The three stages of capture

The following three stages are associated with plane hijacking; however they can be adapted to allow for all cases of capture over a person or position containing hostages.

Stage one: Intimidation—Aggressors intimidate the victims, use force and verbal threats to persuade others to do their bidding. Interestingly, on planes, at this stage the cabin crew will inform the captain via a secret code word which does not seem out of place in normal communication, but will inform the captain of the situation without alerting the hijackers.

HIJACKING

ATTEMPTED HIJACKING: THE HIJACKERS HAVE THREATENED THE PASSENGERS BUT HAVE NOT BREACHED THE CAPTAIN'S CABIN.

HIJACKED: THE HIJACKERS HAVE BREACHED THE FLIGHT DECK.

This type of hidden meaning is what appears to be casual conversation also appears within shinobi literature:

PRIMARY EVIDENCE

If the enemy captures a ninja, takes him close to the gate of his ally and forces him speak as they want, the ninja should let his ally know if his word is true or false by coughing, that is, cough an even number of times if he tells the truth and cough an odd number if its untrue. Further details are to be orally transmitted.
—*The Book of Ninja* (1676)

Make arrangements with the intended receiver beforehand so that you can communicate a meaning with the ways of eye contact, this is one of the primary methods used by kanja *(spies) and shinobi. If you train in this manner, communication can be done at speed.*
—*The Book of Samurai* series (17th century)

Stage two: Custodial—The aggressors have gained total control of the situation. They have removed captured troop weapons, restrained personnel and are now fully in control of a situation. This period has no time scale and depends on the location and availability of help.

In medieval Japan and in the case of the shinobi, the chances of hostage survival was minimal at this stage. Unless a person was a target of interest for ransom or capture, the rest would be put to death. Modern training states that at this time, a cabin crew should do nothing but follow the orders of the hijackers—however airline protocol does say to observe the hijackers for details, clothes, tattoos, distinguishing marks, accents, etc. This applies to other situations that the shinobi engage with and often shinobi have to memorize clothes, armor, banners, color, etc., and have to do so with speed.

Stage three: Resolution—The situation has come to an end, either all hostages are dead, the aims of the attacking group have been met or response teams have neutralized the situation. At this point hidden agents may be left behind and one aggressor may pretend to be a casualty to: further cause injury, increase demoralization to infiltrate a group. This is a classic ninja skill and the use of an attack to actually cover the infiltration of an agent a staple of shinobi skills.

Hostage syndromes

When hostages are exposed to extreme pressure, they may exhibit certain behaviors, these are known as *syndromes*. In the modern world they have been given names and descriptions but do not directly appear in shinobi manuals. However, such conditions would have appeared in old Japan and warriors of old would have witnessed them, even if they did not have a direct description or term to categorize them by. The following syndromes are attributed to hostage situations.

John Wayne Syndrome—A hostage may become extremely depressed and emotional due to not having the ability to help themselves, their loved ones or others in such a situation. They feel powerless and ache to be of service, to be a "hero" in the situation such as John Wayne would have done.

London Syndrome—The hostage verbally attacks the aggressor, trying to call them out and agitating them. They are non-cooperative and argumentative. The name originates from the attack on the Iranian embassy in London in 1980. This is opposite of the Stockholm syndrome.

Stockholm Syndrome—A hostage under extreme emotional stress can develop a bond with their captor. Often, when a threat is removed such as a false execution, a period of extension is "given." The hostage becomes indebted to the captor for unreasonable reasons and bonds are formed.

Escape

People have escaped very difficult situations but also you should remember to be realistic about the situation. Escape is best attempted at the very start of capture. Shoot your way out and be alert at all times. The further into their control you get the harder it is to escape, so escape at the very start or become such a difficult target to acquire it is not worth it. However, be aware if they have the time and resources

TARGET TYPES

SOFT TARGET: A PERSON, PLACE OR SITUATION WHERE SECURITY MEASURES ARE NOT ENFORCED MAKING ATTACK, INFILTRATION, OR DISTURBANCE EASY.

HARD TARGET: A PERSON, PLACE OR SITUATION WITH HIGH LEVELS OF SECURITY MAKING ATTACK DIFFICULT.

and you are specifically their target, then it is a difficult situation to come back from, therefore maintain a "low footprint." Depending on your financial status, it is best to have a hostage rescue policy in place if you visit dangerous areas. There are companies in the world who offer insurance policies for if you are kidnaped and when this happens they will initiate a "snatch back" operation.

Interrogation

Interrogation is a dark art form and can range from simple questions to unspeakable acts of violence and depravity. Today "enhanced interrogation" is a debated topic and its boundaries are blurred between questioning and extreme torture. In the hands of the government its legality is disputed. In the hands of the individual it is illegal, meaning that the security team using these methods on home soil or in enemy territory are always at risk. In old Japan the torturing of "criminals" was not so problematic and the shinobi manuals state that fire torture is of no benefit and that water torture should be used instead.

The five techniques of torture used by the British Government in the 20th century (which are now illegal) were:

1. Stress positions.
2. Hooding so they can see nothing for their time of incarceration.
3. Constant noise.
4. Sleep deprivation.
5. Starvation.

This also included beatings.

To this day the debate about enhanced interrogation continues and it is one reason why the path of the shinobi or modern operative is to step on the horrific path.

You will break

Recognize the fact that you will break. It is a very rare case where someone does not break from prolonged torture. The key is to hold out long enough to render your information useless or to give information that will lead the enemy into a trap. This starts to become the skill of a doomed spy, giving what is thought to be correct information under torture, to confuse or to mislead the enemy. However, remember that a death sentence will normally come at the end of a period of torture during warfare. It is best to become valuable to the enemy such as a double agent if possible. Shinobi knew this and therefore had a backup plan.

Have a back-up plan

Shinobi of old would plan for the eventuality that they would be captured. Fujibayashi-sensei uses the skill of carrying a false letter which is addressed to a well-known commander of the enemy side. This would reveal the enemy general's *supposed* intent to betray their side. The target person used for this should be someone that the enemy forces believe *could* betray them and never be a person famous for their loyalty. Upon reading this letter the enemy would arrest one of their own commanders and then use the shinobi as a double agent and send them back to their own side to work for them with promises of payment. To find the best person to target for this, use a converted spy. Issui-sensei says to use misdirection, such as a love letter for a maid in the castle or house, making the enemy think that you are a love struck individual who is "drunk on love." This will stop them from thinking you are a military threat; however this is mainly for times of peace. In both cases you may either lose your life or be beaten; however, it creates an advantage for the war effort. Therefore create a back-up plan that results in an advantage for the allied side even when it means your own death.

Sleep deprivation

Sleep deprivation does not sound harsh to the average person but it is a well-documented and effective torture technique (some consider it not to be a form of torture). The idea is to stop the target from getting any sleep for days on end and the results are quite drastic. The target—depending on the stage of sleep deprivation—will become totally confused, they will lose most cognitive ability, may hallucinate, have memory loss, create false memories, experience extreme disorientation and above all have a loss of correct judgment It is in this deep place between sleep on consciousness that questions are asked by the enemy because the prisoner no longer has the mental ability to steer their answers in a direction that they wish, pushing them to the edge of this state should get the answers that the questioner wants. This is done by constant attacks when they try to sleep, noise, hunger and movement. The subject is kept awake for very long periods and then allowed to sleep for a very short time but then brutally awakened.

Rape

Rape and gang rape are not only a threat to women; many male captives are also raped. Rape happens in many situations, not just capture. However, rape itself is a form of capture. Continuous rape has been an act of punishment and torture for much of human history and is an unfortunate byproduct of imprisonment.

The use of sex

Operatives may offer sex as a reward for answers or they may use sex to get deeper under cover. This could be with any gender and could mean stepping into a world the agent is not accustomed to. Sex can also be a path to safety inside the enemy. An agent may have sex with a person of power in the enemy ranks which gives them a level of protection.

False executions

False executions are a method of applying extreme psychological torture, the subject is told they will be executed on a certain date or time and believe that their life will truly come to an end at that point, they may even be forced to watch real executions. The point of this is to place the subject under extreme duress and to crack their "spirit." Therefore, the spirit of the commando-spy has to be strong and for that reason, history is full of links between the warriors and religion.

The Spiritual World

The use of God, gods and the spiritual is a subject that requires its own volume and is a theme of infinite interest and relevance. People believe that the spiritual way of war is long behind us, but that is not the case. While wars are now fought in the modern world with logic and intelligence, leaving magic behind, the spiritual aspects still linger on in many forms for a modern army. These include military chaplains, prayers and ceremony. Furthermore, there still exist countless uses of spiritual weapons and practices in developing countries. For the average Western reader, the majority of which come from one of the three major monotheistic religions, the terms, spells, ritual and magic seem redundant but this is not the case. It is subjective to consider a Christian prayer as proper but to think of other religion's prayers as spells. The use of word spell versus prayer is a linguistic shield, both terms are the same to the practitioner. Placing the hands together and reciting the Lord's Prayer is the same as placing the hands in a Buddhist mudra and reciting the ritual of *kuji* for a samurai, it is only the perception of the idea that changes. Writing a quote from the bible on a tank for protection or victory is the same as writing a spell on medieval armor. The terms Crusade and Jihad are obvious in their modern religious connotations; however, the use of ritual and magic in warfare can be identified into the following areas.

Pre-battle Ritual

Magic and ritual that is performed before a force goes to war, this can be broken down into the following points:

- Prayers and offerings
- Magical amulets
- Divination
- Purification
- Sacrifice
- Holy vows
- Ritual decoration
- Ritual performance of the battle and victory

Post-battle Ritual

A ritual which is performed after the victory over the enemy, this can take the following forms:

- Victory dances
- Gloating over the enemy
- Bragging about prowess of self or others
- Frenzied behavior
- The torture of captives as punishment for lost loved ones
- The killing of captives for political gain or revenge
- Cannibalism

Purification Ritual

After battle warriors may often go through purification rituals to dispel the evil of killing, this normally fits into the following:

- Fasting
- Sexual abstinence
- Separation from community
- Sacrifices

The subject of the samurai and the shinobi spirituality plus the comparison to modern warfare rituals is a topic as relevant today as it was in history, in Japan religion in war was extremely strong, from the dawn of the birth of the gods to the divinity of the emperor in the Second World War. The samurai, shinobi and other soldiers both ancient and modern used ritual and magic in warfare and its presence should always be considered in any conflict.

宝永五戊子年十三月

窮源院滴岩了水居士

各三十郎歴也 一水先生也

The death certificate of Natori
Sanjuro Masazumi, the author
of the Shoninki shinobi manual.
His grave can be found at Eunji
Temple in Wakayama, Japan,
where visitors are welcome.

CONCLUSION:
ADAPTING THE NEW AND
PRESERVING THE OLD

*t*he true professionalism of the shinobi of old Japan should now be well established in your mind through the comparison to modern skills. You should also have a better understanding of the darker side of modern military and paramilitary warfare. It has been said that the art of *shinobi no jutsu* should be flexible and should adapt with the times, but this is simply not true.

Historical shinobi arts have a fixed date of termination—they end with the samurai. After the samurai class was abolished, the sub-branch of samurai personnel known as *shinobi no mono* also became redundant and Japan looked to the West as it changed its military. The shinobi did not transform into the modern Japanese spy network and there was no major continuation of military units from samurai to modern era. It was a total upheaval and redefining of the Japanese military, based on Western ideas. In terms of intelligence work the Japanese formed the *Kenpeitai* secret police in the 1880s, a group which ended with the defeat of Japan in World War II.

The Second World War also saw the creation of the now infamous spy school at Nakano, which according to their teaching manifest, only taught a brief overview of *shinobi no jutsu* which lasted about 8 hours, giving their trainees a background in Japanese spying. In 1952 the Japanese formed the Public Security Intelligence Agency (*Koanchosa-cho*) which continues to this day and is Japan's modern intelligence gathering and national espionage agency. The function of the shinobi as a personal spy for the warlords of Japan simply died off with the end of the samurai. Their shinobi teachings—which were already greatly degraded at that time—fell out of history. Therefore, to say that the shinobi arts need to adapt to the modern world is totally incorrect. The shinobi arts are a great cultural asset to Japan but they have their observable boundaries and are locked in time.

Actual modern covert military skills need to adapt to technology and do adapt with great speed. Remembering that principles remain the same, from the birth of the Asian spy in old China all the way to today, we can observe similarities and bring about a comparison between the old and the new. However, actual skillsets will always change depending on the society those skills are used in. The methods and equipment used by the shinobi would not work today, as today's will not work in the future. Therefore, remember that historical shinobi arts are practiced today to cultivate a set of applicable principles and to preserve the teachings of old Japan while modern skills are updated as time passes. It is only as a comparison that we use them here.

As stated at the beginning of this book, the aim of this work is to not only show the historical shinobi community the reality of espionage work in old Japan but also to reveal to those interested in modern special forces the skills and espionage techniques and the high level of professional ability of the shinobi of Japan. This should give the public a more realistic idea of these historical warriors and at the same time allow the casual reader to fully understand the scope of what it means to be an agent at any point in history.

FURTHER READING:
STUDYING THE WAY OF
THE NINJA TODAY

*O*ne question I am often asked is, "where can I study the ways of the shinobi today?" It is difficult to answer this question because there are no existing lineages of *shinobi no jutsu* left and, while there are many people who claim to have historical lineages today, there is not a single one in the world that can produce any proof to back up their claims. I have spent much of my life searching for historical shinobi arts and to this day I have not found a single living tradition that fits into either a historical accurate tradition or carries appropriate proof of claim. The arts of the shinobi should not be taught alone, they should always be displayed as a single part of a larger curriculum of samurai warfare to some degree. Without this there can be no understanding of where the skills of the shinobi fit into the context of Japanese war. If you are searching only for modern applications for the arts of the shinobi, I suggest that you focus on modern Special Forces and spying skills because there are many books on the subject of modern spying and commando tactics. However, for those who wish to fully study the *historical* ways of the shinobi as they were taught in old Japan the best route is to study the scrolls which have been published in English (see pages 184–85); however, in addition to this I have established an organization called Natori-Ryu to allow people to enter into an environment where they can pursue those ancient ways.

Natori-Ryu: The Rebirth of the Samurai and Shinobi

Natori-Ryu was a samurai school of war established in the second half of the 1500s and served the famed warlord Takeda Shingen. Afterwards, the school served the Tokugawa Family and their branch in Wakayama. The school taught samurai and shinobi ways for over 300 years to the samurai of their time. Natori-Ryu's main figure is their 3ʳᵈ grandmaster Natori Sanjuro Masazumi (Issui-sensei) who reorganized the school in the 1600s and incorporated many more elements. The school eventually closed its doors at the end of the 1800s. However, due to the foresight of Issui-sensei, the school's teachings of samurai and shinobi lessons were written down in over 30 scrolls in the 1600s which I have diligently collected from all over Japan and brought together for the first time in over 100 years. This set of scrolls contains a full samurai school of war including some of the most well respected teachings on the shinobi in world today, most notably the famous Shoninki manual now published by Tuttle titled *True Path of the Ninja*.

True Path of the Ninja is the main source of shinobi teachings for Natori-Ryu.

In 2013 a blessing to reopen Natori-Ryu was given by the original Natori family in Wakayama and by Eunji Temple, the resting place of Natori Sanjuro Masazumi. This new version of the school is based on the translations of detailed and annotated scrolls left behind by the grandmasters and students of the school, of which multiple transcriptions exist. The school's teachings are now published in *The Book of Samurai* series which began publication in 2015, with subsequent volumes now being published until the complete school is available in English. Take care not to confuse *The Book of Samurai: the Collected Scrolls of Natori-Ryu* with translations of the scroll known as Hagakure as some publishers have a very similar title. The Hagakure has no connection to Natori-Ryu; however it is still an interesting read and I recommend Tuttle's version which is shown here.

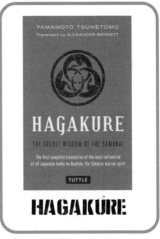

Do not confuse *The Book of Samurai*, which contains the secret teachings of Natori-Ryu, with some versions of the *Hagakure* with similar titles. For those who are also interested in reading the *Hagakure* as well as Issui-sensei's teachings, I recommend Alexander Bennett's *Hagakure: The Secret Wisdom of the Samurai* (Tuttle).

For those who wish to join and enter into training of both samurai and shinobi ways, visit the website www.natori.co.uk and click Natori-Ryu for more information.

Historical Shinobi Scrolls and Research in English

For those who wish to read the translations of the original shinobi scrolls or the most current historical research, the following books constitute my research up to the publication date of this book. I encourage everyone to give historical shinobi some of their time and to keep their fascinating story alive. The books are given in the order that they should be read so that you can build your knowledge of the shinobi arts from the ground up. (Tuttle's *True Path of the Ninja* has already been mentioned above so it will not be included in this section.)

Samurai and Ninja

The first place to start is with Tuttle's *Samurai and Ninja*. This will give you a great foundation for your study of the history and position of the shinobi inside the world of the samurai and a better understanding of the samurai themselves.

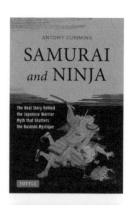

Ninja Skills

Ninja Skills offers a well-illustrated guide to the first 150 lessons you should be focusing on to follow the ways of the shinobi. This is a breakdown of the basic network of ideas that holds shinobi no jutsu together in easy to access lessons.

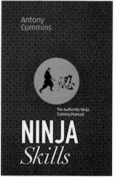

Iga and Koka Ninja Skills

The best direct translation to start with in historical shinobi manuals is *Iga and Koka Ninja Skills*. This is a collection of skills from the famous provinces of Iga and Koka that were written down in the 1700s by Chikamatsu-sensei with the aim of preserving real shinobi teachings. It still stands today as a great way to enter the world of the shinobi scroll.

The Book of Ninja

The Book of Ninja is considered as the "bible" of shinobi scrolls and it deserves this tittle. A colossal volume at over 500 pages it contains a vast amount of teachings and aspects that cover the whole range of shinobi skills. It was written in 1676 by Fujibayashi-sensei in Iga and is considered the standard manual that shinobi after this time from both Iga and Koka used. A student of historical shinobi arts has to study this manual to maintain their knowledge and understanding.

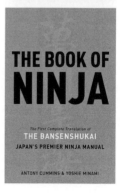

The Secret Traditions of the Shinobi

The Secret Traditions of the Shinobi is one of the more difficult collection of scrolls to read. It contains multiple scrolls by multiple authors, but most importantly it contains Hatori Hanzo's shinobi secrets and one of the earliest shinobi scrolls known to us, the Gunpo Jiyoshu which is considered the most reliable shinobi scroll to date.

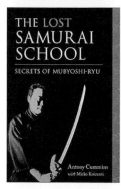

The Lost Samurai School

The Lost Samurai School is the collected teachings of a samurai school known as Mubyoshi-Ryu and contains mainly jujutsu skills and associated samurai combat teachings as well as the mental aspects of the samurai. However, it also contains one of the more famous shinobi scrolls—the Mizukagami—and provides an excellent look at shinobi skills used in civilian life for personal revenge.

In Search of the Ninja

If you have managed to read all of the previous material and for those with a more intellectual slant, the book In Search of the Ninja is a look at the history of the shinobi. It gives a more detailed understanding of their history, from their "birth" to their collapse, including all of the misconceptions and arguments concerning the complex history of the shinobi.

The above volumes form the collection of the major works on the ways and culture of the historical shinobi. For a long time this knowledge was lost to us or had gone through a metamorphosis that transformed the shinobi into the realm of fantasy. While the core of these books is a comparison of old and new, I feel that we, as those interested in clandestine operations throughout history, have a duty to make sure that the history of the shinobi is cared for and preserved for future generations. Your support in this venture will help with the conservation of Japanese culture and history.

The ideograms for the shinobi manual
The Shoninki, translated as *True Path
of the Ninja*. Brushwork is by Monk
Yamamoto of Eunji Temple.

SELECTED BIBLIOGRAPHY

*t*he information pertaining to the history and skills for the shinobi based on my own work have been mentioned in the text and therefore are not listed here, nor are the primary sources as they are well documented in my other works. Information on sword draws has been taken from personal training with Tamiya-Ryu and some modern information has been collected from personal interviews. The following list is a selected list of books used for general information.

All Japan Swordsmith Association. *Introduction to Japanese Swords through Pictures*. Setouchi: All Japan Swordsmith Association, 2006.

Dennen, J. "Ritualized 'Primitive' Warfare and Rituals in War," *Default Journal*, 2005.

Ginsburg, Joannah, et. al. *The Psychology Book*. DK Books, 2012.

Grant, R, G. *Soldier: A Visual History of the Fighting Man*. DK Books, 2007.

Harari, Y. N. *Special Operations in the Age of Chivalry 1100–1550*. Boydell, 2007.

Jarmey, C. *The Concise Book of Muscles*. Lotus, 2003

Jeffery, K. *MI6: The History of the Secret intelligence Service 1909–1949*. Bloomsbury, 2010.

McManners, H. *The Commando Survival Manual—The Practical Guide to Mastering Outdoor Skills and Staying Alive Against The Odds*. DK Publishing, 1994.

Melton, H.K., *The Official C.I.A. Manual of Trickery and Deception*. Hardie Grant, 2009.

Morrison, Bob, Harry Cook, and Bill Mattos. *Extreme Survival—What to Do when Disaster Strikes in the Outdoors, the City and at Home*. Leicester, UK: Hermes House, 2006.

Oman, C. *A History of the Art of War in the Middle Ages: Volume One 378–1278 AD*. Greenhill, 1924.

_____. *A History of the Art of War in the Middle Ages: Volume Two, 1278–1485 AD*. Greenhill, 1924.

Onoda, H. *No Surrender*. Naval Institute Press, 1974.

Pease, A. *Body Language*. Sheldon Press, 1981.

Public Records Office. *S.O.E Syllabus—Lessons in Ungentlemanly Warfare*. PRO, 2001.

Rector, M. *Medieval Combat: A Fifteenth Century Illustrated Manual of Swordfighting and Close Quarter Combat*. Greenhill, 2000.

Sawyer, R. *The Seven Military Classics of Ancient China*. Westview, 1993.

Waterson, J. *The Ismaili Assassins: A History of Medieval Murder*. Frontline, 2008.

Weeks, M. *Heads Up Philosophy*. DK Books, 2014.

Wilson, S.W. *The Book of Five Rings*. Kodansha, 2001.

GLOSSARY

*t*here are many terms used in this book, many of which have been explained within the text; however some of the terms which are used but may be unknown to some have been defined below.

Assassin—a person who kills for political aim or has an agenda and specific target or hired by others who have a political agenda.

Clandestine—keeping something secret or covert and hidden.

Client—the person who hires a spy/security agent.

Espionage—the act of attempting to gain secrets.

ETA—expected time of arrival.

Hard skin—an armored vehicle.

HQ—headquarters.

Iga—an area in Japan famous for producing excellent shinobi. Also see *Koka*.

Iga-mono—a person who is either from the province of Iga or is skilled in the ways of Iga shinobi arts.

Insertion team—a team of locals who help a security team or operator into the target area.

Kanja—a Japanese spy who performs classic spy work. Sometimes interchangeable with ninja, shinobi etc. but in some cases there are slight differences.

Koka—an area in Japan famous for producing excellent shinobi. Also see *Iga*.

Koka mono—a person who is either from the province of Koka or is skilled in the ways of Koka shinobi arts.

Kyojitsu—the concept of substantial and insubstantial, the truth and the lie, falsehood and fact.

Mark—the person being spied upon or who is to be assassinated.

NGO—Non-governmental organization—groups that deal with humanitarian aid and needs in developing countries.

Ninja—a commando—a spy of old Japan—originally known as *shinobi no mono* or just *shinobi*. Also see *shinobi no mono*.

Ninjutsu—see *shinobi no jutsu*.

OP—observation point.

POW—prisoner of war.

Pretext—the cover story used when spying—a false background.

Principle: the person protected by a bodyguard.

Professional assassin—a person whose fulltime occupation is to assassinate .

Propaganda—to use information in an incorrect way to change the minds of others.

Shinobi—see *shinobi no mono*.

Shinobi no jutsu—literally "shinobi skills," it is a term that encompasses the whole teachings of the *shinobi*. The same word is used in *kenjutsu* (swordsmanship), *iaijutsu* (sword quick draw skills) and is present in many forms. It is often used as *ninjutsu* but history shows that *shinobi no jutsu* is correct. It is a set of covert espionage skills used by agents known as *shinobi no mono* (ninja) in old japan.

Shinobi no mono—commonly known as a ninja today, the *shinobi* were a division of a samurai army who dealt with espionage and covert operations. They are similar to the *kanja* (classic spies) and were taken from all levels of society's social classes. It most likely started as a job taken on by skilled men but later became a fulltime profession.

Soft skin—a normal vehicle without armor.

ABOUT THE AUTHOR

A ntony Cummins is an author and historical researcher. He concentrates on investigating and disseminating the history of the Japanese *shinobi*. Taking on the role of project manager and producer, Antony, with the *Historical Ninjutsu Research Team*, has translated and published multiple *shinobi* and *samurai* manuals including *The Book of Ninja, Book of Samurai, Iga and Koka Ninja Skills, Secret Traditions of the Shinobi, True Path of the Ninja, The Lost Samurai School* and *Samurai War Stories*. He has also published his own work on the samurai and shinobi: *In Search of the Ninja, Samurai and Ninja* and *Ninja Skills*. He has also written *The Dark Side of Japan*, a look at the darker side of folklore. He has appeared in the TV documentaries *Samurai Head Hunters, Ninja Shadow Warriors, Samurai Warrior Queens, The 47 Ronin* and *Ninja*. For more information about Antony Cummins and his team see current social media sites and his website www.natori.co.uk.

Antony also leads the resurrection of the *samurai* school of war Natori-Ryu. Further information can be found at the above website.

About the Illustrator

J ayson Kane was born in South Africa and studied Art, Design and Print Making in Manchester, UK. His hobbies include playing and recording music, illustration, and design.

Having worked with Antony Cummins for many years, his portfolio includes *True Path of The Ninja* (cover concept designer), *The Secret Traditions of the Shinobi* (front cover designer), *Iga and Koka Ninja Skills* (internal illustrations), *The Illustrated Guide to Viking Martial Arts* (internal illustrations), *The Lost Warfare of India: An Illustrated Guide* (front cover designer) and *Ninja Skills* (internal illustrations).